Bread & Yeast Cookery

DAVID & CHARLES

Newton Abbot London

British Library Cataloguing in Publication Data
Bread & yeast cookery.—(David & Charles Kitchen Workshop)
  1. Bread   2. Yeast   3. Cookery
  641.8′15   TX769

ISBN 0-7153-8457-0

© Illustrations: A/S Hjemmet 1979
   Text: David & Charles 1983

Typeset by MS Filmsetting Ltd, Frome, Somerset
and printed in The Netherlands
by Smeets Offset BV, Weert
for David & Charles (Publishers) Limited
Brunel House, Newton Abbot, Devon

The Ingredients and the Oven

Bread is an important part of our diet. It contains the proteins we need, and the coarser the bread is the more beneficial it is for our teeth, our digestion, in fact for our whole body.

Freshly baked sweet cakes may simply melt in your mouth, but they are nowhere near so wholesome.

There are many advantages in doing your own baking; it is both cheap and good, and there are many more possibilities of varying the types of bread. Bread baking once or twice a week can be fitted into the working routine of almost everyone. The actual baking is enjoyable too, not to mention the delicious smell which pervades the kitchen.

It pays to make large quantities while you are at it. The work is about the same and you save electricity by making full use of a hot oven.

Read about large-quantity baking on pages 60–1, and how to freeze bread on pages 62–3.

About Baking

Bread is usually made of yeast, flour, salt and liquid, but there is great scope for variation by using different types of flour and by the addition of different flavours.

Here is some information regarding different ingredients and their properties.

Yeast

Yeast consists of living, microscopic cells which develop when liquid, carbohydrates and protein are added. During this development process carbon dioxide is liberated, causing the dough to rise. The ideal temperature for the yeast cells is between 27°C (80°F) and 30°C (85°F). If the temperature is lower, it takes longer for the dough to rise. For cold rising, only half the amount of yeast is used and all the ingredients should be kept at 10°C (50°F). In the refrigerator, rising will then take approximately 8 hr. If the temperature in the dough rises to over 37°C (100°F), the rising takes place too quickly and the baked product will have large irregular holes. At 50–55°C (120–130°F) the yeast cells die and the dough will not rise. Yeast may be bought fresh or as granulated (dried) yeast. Fresh yeast is soft, smooth and greyish white in colour. A white coating on fresh yeast does not affect its leavening properties, but stale yeast with cracks and brown edges should not be used.

There are two methods for using dried yeast. One is to dissolve it in liquid; the other is to mix it in directly with the flour. Follow the directions on the packet or tin.

Fresh yeast can only be kept for a limited time and must be kept in the refrigerator. It may be frozen but must be thawed out before it is used. Dried yeast will keep for a long time, provided it is kept in a cool dry place and the packet, or preferably the tin, is kept tightly closed after use.

Sourdough

In the old days, sourdough was used all the time. A lump of dough from baking day was kept in a cool place to be used for the next baking. This is an excellent procedure, which can well be used today in households where baking is done regularly. The sourdough is stirred into the liquid being added to the dough at the next baking, possibly with the addition of a little new, fresh yeast.

Sourdough can be made by stirring flour and water or sour milk together. By natural fermentation, after 24–48 hr the sourdough is ready to use.

Liquid
Water, buttermilk, fresh or sour milk, or beer, are customarily used for yeast baking. The temperature must not be over 37°C (100°F) for the sake of the yeast cells. The whole dough will then have a temperature of approximately 25–30°C (80–85°F). Bread and cakes made with milk will not be as light as if they were made with water, but neither will they dry out as quickly.

Fats
A little butter, margarine, oil or other fat in the dough will keep all kinds of bread fresh longer. Small amounts of fat can be melted into the dough liquid but, if a lot of butter is called for in the recipe, this should be crumbled into the flour or rolled into the dough after it has risen once.

Flour
Wheat flour, of all the various types of flour, is the most suitable for baking and therefore is often mixed with other flours. When wheat flour is mixed with liquid at the right temperature, gluten is formed, gluten being an elastic substance which binds the carbon dioxide freed by the yeast. The viscous gluten threads hold the dough together, the starch in the flour fills it out and the yeast makes it rise. The degree of moisture in flour varies and consequently its capacity to absorb moisture. Therefore always hold back a little of the flour until

you see how much liquid is being absorbed. The dough should just leave the sides of the bowl clean. If you use too much flour the bread will be hard and dull when baked.

Eggs
Eggs vary a great deal in size, but a standard egg weighs 55–65g (2–2¼oz) or Grade 3 or 4. In recipes where the number of eggs is given, if nothing else is mentioned, Grade 3 or 4 eggs are intended. Eggs which are to be used for brushing over the top of buns or bread made with yeast may be beaten with a little milk to make them go farther when large quantities are being baked.

How to Use the Oven
Most ovens have thermostats, but these are not always entirely accurate. If there is any deviation between the temperature and baking time given in a recipe and that which is registered on your own oven, make a note on this beside each recipe. Oven heat and baking time are different for large loaves of bread, small rolls, cakes, buns etc. If The main rule is that small things are baked at higher temperatures than large things. Large loaves and cakes are placed low down in the oven, small rolls and buns etc are baked on the middle rack.

When loaves and cakes have risen completely they should be brushed with beaten egg etc or sprinkled with seeds or flour according to the recipe. Start heating your oven when the dough has finished rising for the first time, then it will be at the right temperature when the dough has finished rising for the

second time.
Bread continues to rise for a while after it has been put in the oven. In order to avoid too hard a crust forming at once, a saucer filled with warm water may be placed on the bottom of the oven. The crust will be extra crisp if the bread is brushed with water a few times during the baking.

Oven Temperatures	°C	°F	Gas
Cool	110	225	
Cool	120	250	½
Very slow	140	275	1
Slow	150	300	2
Moderately slow	160	325	3
Moderate	180	350	4
Moderately hot	190	375	5
Moderately hot	200	400	6
Hot	220	425	7
Very hot	230	450	8
Very hot	240	475	9
Extremely hot	260	500	

Measuring and Weighing
Although it might seem easier and quicker to use a measure, weighing the ingredients gives a very much more accurate result. However, standard measuring spoons can be purchased as sets. The spoonfuls should always be level to give the correct measurement.

It is not always necessary to weigh butter or margarine for baking as a small error either way will not make much difference. Divide the packet as accurately as you can with a sharp knife.

Keeping and Freezing
Instructions on keeping and freezing bread and cakes made of yeast dough are to be found on pages 62–3.

When You Bake . .

Bread made from fermenting dough has been known for thousands of years. But it was only two or three centuries ago in England that yeast, as an ingredient, came to be used to speed up the successful but time-consuming sourdough method, with its slow leavening. At one time women made yeast at home from hops or beer leavings – with very variable results. Nowadays most bread comes from large commercial concerns, but more and more people are making at least some of their own. For reasons of both taste and healthy eating, they want to try out the different flours available from the coarsest rye to the lightest white.

The baking of bread and cakes of yeast dough is a craft, and practice and more practice is necessary to get a good result. There are tricks to be learned, but once you get the hang of it, there is nothing to it. Even though the recipes in this book on yeast baking are as exact as possible, you can be unlucky, and below are tips and advice on yeast baking in general. Don't be discouraged if the result the first time isn't quite what you hoped for – perhaps the flour was a little too cold, even that can be enough to rob you of success.

10 Good Tips

1 Let all the ingredients you are going to use stand at room temperature in the kitchen for a couple of hours. Even a cold bowl can cool the dough sufficiently to prevent rising taking place as it should.

2 Yeast dough mustn't stand at too low a temperature or in a draught, either when it is being kneaded or while it is rising.

3 Never introduce yeast to salt or sugar on their own. It should be dissolved in tepid or room-temperature liquid. If you mix yeast directly into the flour, both the yeast and the flour should have stood for a couple of hours in the kitchen.

4 If you have a food mixer which is powerful enough to be used for yeast doughs, only half the flour should be added together with the other ingredients. Do not let the machine knead for more than 3–5 min at a time. If you let it knead longer, the dough will not rise properly. The rest of the flour can be kneaded in by hand.

5 In a recipe using both coarse and fine flour, the coarse should be added first and the fine afterwards. Do not add all the flour at once, for flour does not absorb moisture equally at all times. Absorption can vary according to the moisture in the flour after being stored etc.

6 The oven should always be heated in advance to the desired temperature before the bread or cakes are put in, unless otherwise indicated in the recipe.

7 Baked bread, when ready to be taken out of the oven, gives a special hollow sound which is easily recognisable when you tap on the bottom of the loaf with your fingers. Bread which is baked in a tin should preferably be taken out of the tin and baked on the oven rack or a baking sheet for the last 10–15 min.

8 Bread and cakes should normally be cooled on a rack. This releases the steam and the baked product keeps dry. Certain breads (especially the coarse types) can be cooled under a cloth to obtain a softer crust and consistency.

9 Preferably use a timer when you are baking and while the yeast dough is rising. Make a note on your recipes if the temperatures and times given do not correspond with your stove.

10 Do not open the oven door too early and on no account let it bang shut when you close it, as the resulting draught is enough to cause the bread or cakes to collapse.

If you should be Unlucky...

The dough did not rise properly
The liquid was too warm – or too cold.
The dough was standing in a draught.
The yeast was too old, and had become dry or crumbled.

The dough collapsed
The dough was left to rise too long the second time.

The bread has big or irregular holes
The dough was not kneaded enough after the first rising.

The bread is hard
Too much flour in the dough.
The dough did not rise properly.

The bread is heavy
Too little flour in the dough.
The dough did not rise enough or the temperature was too warm during the rising period.

The bread is cracked
The dough rose too quickly.
The dough should have been pierced or cut into.

Grain Becomes Flour

Bread has always made up a considerable part of our daily food, and experience has shown that grain products make a good basis for general well-being, health and working capacity. For many thousands of years man has cultivated grain. Formerly it was a condition for permanent settlement, for grain made people independent of a vagrant roaming existence with its constant hunting for, and collecting of, food. Well-filled storehouses of grain provided security against bad years and famine.

In Europe as a whole, the principal grains used are oats, wheat and rye. In Great Britain, wheat is the staple grain in the diet and, in one form or another, the constituent of most breads and cakes. On the Continent, however, rye is an important cereal for bread making.

The most important part of the grain plant is the grain itself. It consists of the husk (bran), the germ and the endosperm (starch).

The husk makes up 15 per cent of the weight of the grain and protects the germ. The latter is just inside the husk and makes up only some 3 per cent of the weight.

The endosperm is the main part of the grain. It makes up around 82 per cent of the weight.

The ripe grain contains elements from all the main groups of foodstuffs:

   the energy-providing carbohydrates
   proteins and fats
   minerals
   vitamins.

Flours used in Yeast Baking

The names for commercially produced breads, indicating what flour was used in the baking, are numerous. Basically home-baking bread flours, except for oatmeal – a regional speciality – are as follows:

Plain (white) flour made from wheat
Rye flour (mixed with wheat)
Wheatmeal flour
Wholemeal flour
Wholegrain rye flour

These, on their own, or in various combinations, provide a fascinating variety of breads, cakes and pastries with yeast as the raising agent.

How is Flour Made?

Any number of different kinds of flour can be made, but two main groups are distinguishable, namely *refined flour* and *whole-ground flour*. Refined flour is made from the starchy part of the grain. The husk and the germ are sifted away, and the flour is very light or white in colour.

Whole-ground flour is made by crushing the entire grain, and it contains both the husk, the germ and the kernel. Nothing is removed in the grinding process.

The term fine and coarse refers to whether the grain is finely or coarsely crushed, but both contain the whole grain with the husk, the germ and the kernel.

Wheat Flour

Wheat flour is the type of flour most often used in Great Britain. It is used alone or mixed with other types. Its baking properties are improved when the flour is stored for a while after it is ground, as the flour needs time to mature.

Plain (white) flour has a low extraction rate, something like 70 per cent, meaning that little except starch is left, the husk and the germ are largely discarded. It is also bleached. Ordinary plain flour, while best for other forms of baking, lacks the gluten desirable for making bread, though it gives a tolerably good result. Strong plain flour, from wheat grown in extreme climates such as Canada and the United States and containing more gluten, is far better and should be used if possible.

Wheatmeal (brown) flours have an extraction rate of about 85–90 per cent and are flours with the bran partly removed. They produce a lighter, moister loaf than wholewheat flours. You should make sure an extraction rate is given on the packet, otherwise what you buy as

brown flour could be white flour coloured.

The terms wholemeal and wholewheat are, to a large extent, synonymous, being better differentiated by the coarseness and method of the milling. Stone-ground flour, for instance, is coarse with a distinct flavour, and milled in the old way between millstones instead of roller milled.

Wholemeal and wholewheat flours are of 100 per cent extraction, ie the whole of the wheat grain is used.

Rye Flour

Rye has weaker baking properties than wheat and for this reason 15 per cent wheat flour is added to it to improve its baking properties. The various kinds of flour are mixed with each other to create variation in baking products, but wheat flour is the essential element due to its excellent baking properties.

Storing Flour

As a general rule flour should be kept in a dry, cool place well away from strong-smelling food.

Keeping value is dependent on the amount of water in the flour but, on the whole, flour may well be considered a non-perishable type of food. Under proper storage conditions wheat and rye flours can be kept up to two years without deteriorating in quality. Wholewheat flours have a much shorter life than white flours because the germ retained in the wholewheat contains fat which can become rancid. It also normally keeps a shorter time in summer than in winter. The best containers are an enamel bin or jars with tight-fitting lids. When you buy flour, the wrapping is always of paper. Paper allows the water vapour to escape and prevents the flour from forming lumps; nevertheless, for the best result, flour should be sifted before being added in as directed in a particular recipe. Some brands of flour are much finer than others at the point of sale.

Sacks of grain and flour – we have many possibilities to choose from when we start to bake. Mixing coarse and fine types provides any number of variations of bread, cakes and buns.

Working with Yeast

Baking with yeast may be divided into the following steps – dough making, rising, airing, kneading and forming, second rising and, finally, baking. This book contains recipes for all kinds of breads and cakes, but first we shall deal with the basic recipes for the most usual types of bread and go thoroughly through the two most usual methods.

Everyday Bread (basic recipe)
50g (2oz) yeast
250ml (9fl oz) water
25g (1oz) butter
2 × 5ml tsp (2tsp) salt
250g (9oz) rye flour
250g (9oz) strong plain flour
suitable for freezing

Brush with water and prick before baking.
Bake for about 50 min at 200°C, 400°F, Gas 6.

Kneipp Bread (basic recipe)
25g (1oz) yeast
250 ml (9fl oz) water
1–2 × 5ml tsp (1–2tsp) salt
2 × 15ml tbsp (2tbsp) oil
100g (¼lb) rye flour
125g (4½oz) wholemeal flour

Brush with water and prick.
Bake for about 40 min at 200°C, 400°F, Gas 6.

Whole-grain Bread (basic recipe)
50g (2oz) yeast
300ml (½pt) boiling water
2 × 5ml tsp (2tsp) salt
1 × 15ml tbsp (1tbsp) butter
150g (5oz) stone-ground wholewheat flour
50g (2oz) rye flour
about 250g (9oz) strong plain flour
50g (2oz) whole grains

Put 25g (1oz) grain to soak in the boiling water for about 2 hr. Add to the dough. Sprinkle 25g (1oz) grain on top of the loaf. Brush with water and make a few cuts on top.
Bake for about 40 min at 200°C, 400°F, Gas 6.

Graham Bread (basic recipe)
50g (2oz) yeast, 300ml (½pt) milk
50g (2oz) butter or margarine
1 × 5ml tsp (1tsp) salt
1 × 5ml tsp (1tsp) sugar
350g (¾lb) wholemeal flour
180g (6½oz) strong plain flour

Use a 1kg (2lb) loaf tin. Brush with water and prick before baking.
Bake for about 30 min at 200°C, 400°F, Gas 6.

Homemade Bread (basic recipe)
50g (2oz) yeast
1 × 15ml tbsp (1tbsp) oil
1 × 5ml tsp (1tsp) salt
½ litre (about 1pt) skimmed milk
250g (9oz) stone-ground wholewheat flour
250g (9oz) rye flour
250g (9oz) strong plain flour

1 The crumbled fresh yeast or the dried yeast is put in a hollow in the flour.

2 Dissolve the yeast in the tepid liquid, and stir in a little of the flour to make a pre-dough.

3 The pre-dough should look like this when it has risen for about 15 min.

4 Add seasonings and melted, cooled butter or other fat.

5 Stir the dough vigorously so that it becomes shiny and smooth.

Brush with sweetened coffee and cut a deep slit lengthwise.

Bake in a 1kg (2lb) loaf tin at 200 °C, 400 °F, Gas 6 for about 1 hr.

Method 1

1 When baking with yeast, it is worth stressing again that all ingredients and equipment must be at room temperature. If, for example, the flour is too cold, the dough will rise slowly and poorly. Therefore, let everything be ready in the room a couple of hours before baking.

Always sift the flour; not only will it be lighter, the temperature will be even.

The amount of flour in any particular recipe can never be given entirely accurately, as the amount of moisture in flour varies; but it is a good rule not to use all the flour to begin with and then add more if necessary. This way, you should be able to avoid too dry a dough.

Make a hollow in the flour and put in the crumbled fresh or dried yeast.

2 Warm milk or water until it is lukewarm (about 35 °C, 95 °F). If it is more than a few degrees warmer than 45 °C (113 °F), the yeast cells will be killed and the dough will not rise. It is better to dissolve the yeast in too cold a liquid than too warm. Pour the liquid slowly over the yeast and stir in a little of the flour. Sprinkle a thin layer of flour over the top, cover the bowl with a cloth or large polythene bag and let it stand in a warm, draught-free place for about 15 min.

3 When this pre-dough has finished rising, there will be cracks in the flour which was sprinkled on top. The flour below will have the same temperature as the yeast misture, and this is important for the rising.

4 Melt the butter and let it cool until it has the same temperature as the other ingredients. Then add salt and eggs, sugar and other flavour ingredients if the dough is to be used for cakes. If the butter amount is greater than 10–15 per cent of the flour, the butter should be rubbed into the flour before the liquid is poured in. In some recipes, however, cold butter is rolled into the dough after the first rising.

5 Stir the dough thoroughly until it is smooth and elastic. If you are using a food mixer with a dough hook, add only half the flour and do not let the machine run for more than 3–5 min. Then work the rest of the flour into the dough on the baking board. Place the dough on a floured board and knead it thoroughly. Hold onto the dough with one hand and pull it out with the other. Just before the gluten threads snap, knead the dough together into a clump again. Repeat this until the dough no longer clings to the board or to your hands.

6 Put the dough back into the bowl, cover it and put it in a warm place, away from any draught. Yeast dough must never stand in a draught and never be placed on any direct heat, unless this is stated specifically in the recipe. You can sprinkle a thin layer of flour over the bowl to prevent a dry film from forming. If the yeast dough is oily, a cloth can be moistened and wrung out and placed on top. Or put the bowl in a polythene bag. The dough has finished rising when it has doubled in bulk. Transfer it to the baking board, press it with the flat of your hand and knead it lightly.

7 If the dough is to be divided, do this now, and let the portions stand for 3–5 min before you begin to work with them. This allows the elastic gluten threads to contract, so that the dough is easier to roll out. If, for example, you have divided the dough into three to make braided bread, hold the strips up for a moment by one end. Then the pieces of dough will not contract when they are rolled out. If no other procedure is mentioned in the recipe, the dough should be put to rise again in a tin or on a baking sheet for about 20 min. Before it is put in the oven, it should be brushed over, slit, sprinkled etc, according to the recipe.

8 Bread and large cakes should be baked on the lowest rack in the oven; buns and rolls in the middle. If you use greaseproof paper on the baking sheet or in the tin, it is not necessary to grease the sheet or tin as well. The paper will not stick and it can be used several times. It also simplifies cleaning.

Bread and cakes cooked in tins can be taken out of the tin and placed directly on the baking sheet for the last 10–15 min if the bottom and sides are too light in colour. Tap the bread with your finger – if there is a

---

6 After the dough has been allowed to rise for about 15 mins, it should look like this, plump and springy.

7 Twine three long 'sausages' of dough into braided dough. Fold the ends in under the bread.

8 The bread rises for the second time, is brushed (with egg etc), and put in the pre-heated oven until baked.

hollow sound, it is baked through. Place the baked bread or cake on a wire rack. This lets the steam come out and the bread will not be damp on the bottom.

If the bread or cake is to be frozen, wrap it in freezer foil while it is lukewarm, and put it in the freezer when it is completely cold. This way the crust will not fall off when thawing is done. Bread and cakes can be thawed out in their wrapping at room temperature, but buns and rolls should be thawed and warmed in the oven at 200°C, 400°F, Gas 6.

Method 2

In this method we start by dissolving the yeast in cold or lukewarm liquid. If the dough is to have a cold rising, use cold liquid, but if you want it to rise as quickly as possible, use lukewarm. The method is equally good for all types of yeast baking. The illustrations opposite show the dissolved yeast being poured into the flour, but sometimes a large bowl is used at the start to dissolve

the yeast in and the flour etc added to the yeast.

White Bread (basic recipe)

(makes 1 large loaf or 24 rolls)
Preparation time: 15 min
Rising time: about 15 min
Baking time and oven temperature: bread, 35 min at 200°C, 400°F, Gas 6; dinner rolls, 12–18 min at 220–240°C, 425–475°F, Gas 7–9
Put large loaf on the lowest rack and dinner rolls on the middle rack in the oven
Suitable for freezing

15g (½oz) yeast
2 × 5ml tsp (2tsp) salt
15g (½oz) butter or margarine
300ml (½pt) water or milk
about ½kg (1lb) strong plain flour

1 Heat the water or milk to 35–37°C (95–100°F), and melt the butter in the liquid or crumble it into the flour. Dissolve the crumbled yeast in the liquid and add salt and most of the flour. Work the

dough thoroughly with a wooden spoon or in an electric mixer, and knead in the rest of the flour with your hands. Cover the dough, put it in a warm place and let it rise for about 30–40 min.

2 Take out the dough and knead well on a floured board. Shape into a large loaf or 24 dinner rolls and let them rise again under a cover for 10–20 min.

3 Brush over with cream, milk or beaten egg and slit the loaf with a sharp knife. Dinner rolls may also be slit, but this is only for decoration (see illustrations, page 16).

4 Allow about 35 min baking time at 200°C, 400°F, Gas 6 for a large loaf made with this basic dough; for rolls, 12–18 min at 220–240°C, 425–475°F, Gas 7–9. The oven should be heated in advance before the rolls are put in. A large loaf should be baked on the lowest rack, rolls on the middle rack of the oven. This basic dough can be used for unsweetened buns, crescents etc as well as for white bread and rolls.

Time-table for Freshness

For all recipes the time you need for baking is given. If you want to serve baked products as fresh as possible, count back from the time you want to serve them, subtract time for cooling, baking, rising and preparation, and you will arrive at the exact time you should start. This applies particularly to baked items such as kringels, buns, crescents etc, which can be served warm.

Yeast Dough Step by Step

1 Sprinkle dried yeast or fresh, crumbled yeast into lukewarm liquid (35–37°C, 95–100°F) and stir well. It is simplest to dissolve the yeast in a little of the liquid, then add the remaining liquid afterwards. A white film on fresh yeast does not affect its rising properties, but if the yeast is dried out, cracked and has brown edges, it should be thrown away.

2 Mix together most of the flour, salt and any other seasonings; add the dissolved yeast and work the dough thoroughly together. An electric mixer with a dough hook may also be used for 3 min at low speed.

3 Add the rest of the flour, a little at a time, and continue to knead the dough with your hands. The butter may be melted with the liquid or be rubbed into the last portion of flour before it is kneaded into the dough.

4 Remove the dough to a floured board. Hold it with one hand to the board, and pull it away from you with the other hand. Just before the 'threads' of the dough snap, form it again into a clump. Repeat this until the dough is firm and not sticky.

5 Make the flexible dough into a ball and put it into a bowl or tin. Sprinkle a thin layer of flour on top. Cover with a clean cloth or polythene, and put the dough in a draught-free but not too warm place until it has doubled in bulk. The rising time is dependent on the kind of flour used, on whether the liquid is lukewarm or cold, and whether there is fat in the dough.

6 Remove the dough to a floured baking sheet, and press it flat with your hands. Knead lightly and form it into the shape you want. Place it in a tin or on a greased baking sheet and leave to rise again in a draught free place, at room temperature, until well risen. Brush the top, score it and bake according to the recipe.

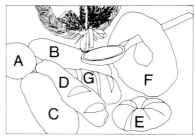

A *Round Caraway-seed Bread (p 17)*
B *Bran Bread (below)*
C *Wholemeal Bread (p 18)*
D *Farmer's Bread (p 17)*
E *Coarse Round Bread (p 16)*
F *Rye-flour Ring (p 16)*
G *White Bread (p 12)*

Wholemeal Bread

The coarser types of bread contain important nutrients and fibres necessary to our bodies.

Bran Bread

(makes 2 loaves)
Preparation time: 15–20 min
Rising time: about 1 hr
Baking time: about 40 min
Oven temperature: 200°C, 400°F, Gas 6
Lowest rack in the oven
Suitable for freezing

75g (3oz) yeast
½ litre (about 1pt) lukewarm water
1 × 15ml tbsp (1tbsp) salt
200g (7oz) wheat bran
½kg (1lb 2oz) rye flour
about 300g (11oz) strong plain flour

1 Dissolve the yeast in lukewarm water and add salt, most of the wheat bran, rye flour and a little of the plain flour. Knead well and add more white flour.
2 Let the dough stand, covered, in a warm place to rise for about 40 min. Knead the dough lightly and add more plain flour if necessary. Divide the dough in two and let it stand a little. Form it into oblong loaves.
3 Leave the loaves to rise again on the baking sheet for about 20 min. Brush them with water, milk, cream or melted butter and sprinkle the rest of the wheat bran on top.
4 Bake the loaves as directed, and place on a wire rack until cold.

15

Linseed Bread

Coarse Round Bread

Farmer's Bread

When you have brushed the bread, score it before putting it in the oven. By doing this some of the carbon dioxide collected in the bread can escape during baking, and so prevents cracking.
Use a sharp knife, dip it in flour and lightly score the top. Above are different ways of scoring bread.

Linseed Bread

(makes 2 loaves)
Preparation time: 15–20 min
Rising time: about 2 hr
Oven temperature: 220°C, 425°F, Gas 7
Middle rack in the oven
Suitable for freezing

75g (3oz) yeast
¾ litre (about 1¼pt) lukewarm water
1kg (about 2¼lb) rye flour
1 × 15ml tbsp (1tbsp) salt
3 × 15ml tbsp (3tbsp) linseed
2 × 15ml tbsp (2tbsp) caraway seeds
about 200g (7oz) strong plain flour

1 Dissolve the crumbled yeast in 100ml (4fl oz) lukewarm water, add remaining water, most of the rye flour, salt, linseed and caraway seeds. Knead the dough until it becomes elastic with the rest of the rye flour and as much plain flour as is necessary to prevent the dough from sticking to the bowl.
2 Place the dough, covered, in a warm place and let it rise for about 1½ hr. Knead and form it into two round loaves which are then scored in a diamond pattern. Let these rise again for 20–30 min on a baking sheet, then brush with water.
3 Place a fireproof pan with water in the bottom of the oven and put the loaves on the middle rack. If the loaves become too brown, the temperature should be lowered near the end of the baking time, or the loaves covered with greaseproof paper or foil.
4 Brush the baked loaves with lukewarm water and cool on a wire rack with a cloth on top.

Rye-flour Rings

(makes 2 rings)
Preparation time: 15–20 min
Rising time: about 1 hr
Baking time: about 50 min
Oven temperature: 200°C, 400°F, Gas 6
Lowest rack in the oven
Suitable for freezing

50g (2oz) butter
½ litre (about 1pt) lukewarm water
50g (2oz) yeast
1 × 15ml tbsp (1tbsp) salt
½kg (1lb 2oz) fine whole-grain rye flour
250g (9oz) rye flour
250g (9oz) strong plain flour

1 Melt the butter in the lukewarm water and dissolve the crumbled yeast in the mixture. Add salt, fine whole-grain rye flour and rye flour and knead the dough well. Add enough plain flour to make a firm, elastic consistency.
2 Divide the dough into two portions, roll them out into 'sausages', and make a ring out of each. Lay them on the baking sheet, cover them with a cloth, and let them rise for about 1 hr in a warm place. (The rings only need to rise once.)
3 Brush the rings with water, sprinkle a little rye flour over them and bake as directed. Cool on a wire rack under a cloth.

Coarse Round Bread

(makes 2 loaves)
Preparation time: 20 min + 2 hr for soaking the whole wheat
Rising time: about 1¼ hr
Baking time: about 40 min
Oven temperature: 200°C, 400°F, Gas 6
Lowest rack in the oven
Suitable for freezing

75g (3oz) crushed whole wheat grains
50g (2oz) butter
½ litre (about 1pt) skimmed milk
about 100g (¼lb) cottage cheese
50g (2oz) yeast
1 × 15ml tbsp (1tbsp) salt
300g (11oz) rye flour
about 700g (1½lb) strong plain flour

1 Pour hot water over the crushed wheat grains and let them soak for 2 hr. The water must not be boiling.
2 Melt the butter, add the milk, and be sure that the mixture is not warmer than 37°C (100°F). Stir in the cottage cheese and pour a little of the mixture over the crumbled yeast.
3 Add salt, the drained crushed wheat, the remaining liquid and the rye flour, and stir well. Knead the dough with plain flour until it becomes elastic and no longer sticks to the bowl. Cover, place in a warm place, and let it rise for about 50 min.
4 Divide the dough into two and let both parts stand for about 5 min. Make a ball out of each lump of dough, flatten it and put it to rise on the baking sheet for about 20 min. Brush with milk, cream or melted

butter and cut a star with a sharp knife (cut deepest in the middle). Bake the round loaves as directed and cool them on a wire rack.

Round Caraway-seed Bread

(makes 2 loaves)
Preparation time: about 20 min
Rising time: about 1 hr
Baking time: 35–40 min
Oven temperature: 200°C, 400°F, Gas 6
Lowest rack in the oven
Suitable for freezing

50g (2oz) yeast
½ litre (about 1 pt) buttermilk
100ml (4fl oz) lukewarm water
1 × 15ml tbsp (1tbsp) salt
4–5 × 15ml tbsp (4–5tbsp) crushed whole wheat grains
600g (about 1¼lb) rye flour
about 300g (11oz) strong plain flour

1 Dissolve the yeast in the lukewarm water and add the buttermilk (at room temperature), salt, the crushed whole wheat grains and most of the rye flour. Knead the dough thoroughly and add the rest of the rye flour. Knead the dough again with as much of the strong plain flour as needed to make it elastic.
2 Let the dough stand covered in a warm place for about 40 min. Knead lightly and form it into two round loaves. Leave them to rise on a baking sheet for about 20 min.
3 Cut a slash across the loaves and brush them with milk, cream or melted butter before baking as directed. Place the loaves on wire rack until they are cold.

Farmer's Bread

(makes 2 loaves)
Preparation time: 20 min
Rising time: about 1¼ hr
Baking time: about 30 min
Oven temperature: 220°C, 425°F, Gas 7
Lowest rack in the oven
Suitable for freezing

50g (2oz) yeast
200ml (7fl oz) lukewarm water
400ml (¾pt) buttermilk
1 × 15ml tbsp (1tbsp) salt
50g (2oz) coarse rye flour
250g (9oz) wholemeal flour
250g (9oz) rye flour
about 400g (14oz) strong plain flour

Linseed Bread – extremely good for you, and tasty too.

1 Dissolve the yeast in the lukewarm water and add lukewarm buttermilk, salt, rye flours and wholemeal flour.
Knead the dough well and add enough plain flour so that it no longer sticks to the bowl.
2 Let the dough stand, covered, in a warm place for about 45 min.

Divide it into two and let the two portions stand for 3–4 min. Roll them out to two oblong loaves and let them rise again on the baking sheet for about 30 min.
3 Brush the loaves with coffee, milk or cream. Cut diagonal slashes across their tops and bake as directed. Place on a wire rack until cold.

Wholemeal Bread (2 loaves)

Preparation time: 20 min + 2 hr for soaking the whole grain
Rising time: about 1¼ hr
Baking time: about 40 min
Oven temperature: 200–220°C, 400–425°F, Gas 6–7
Lowest rack in the oven
Suitable for freezing

75g (3oz) whole wheat grains
75g (3oz) yeast
600ml (about 1pt) water
1 × 15ml tbsp (1tbsp) salt
2 × 15ml tbsp (2tbsp) melted butter
400g (14oz) stone-ground wholewheat flour
about ½kg (1lb 2oz) strong plain flour

1 Pour warm water over the whole grain and let stand for 2 hr. The water must not be boiling.

2 Dissolve the crumbled yeast in 100ml (4fl oz) lukewarm water and add salt, the remaining water, the melted butter, the wholewheat flour and the drained whole grains. Stir until the dough is elastic and add the plain flour.

3 Let the dough stand, covered, in a warm place for about 45 min. Take it out of the bowl and divide it into two portions. Let them stand for a few minutes. Flatten them and roll them loosely together diagonally into two oblong loaves. Leave to rise for 20–25 min on a baking sheet.

4 Sprinkle a little flour on the loaves and bake them as directed. Put a cloth over them when they have finished baking and leave on a wire rack until cold.

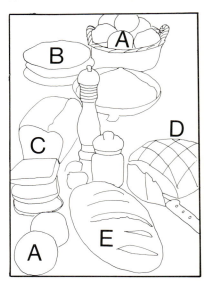

What should a loaf of bread look like? Loaves don't all have to be oblong, just look at the selection shown here:
A Crusty Rolls
B Coriander Bread (page 33)
C Health Bread
D Ham Bread, E Yoghurt Bread.

Ham Bread

(makes 1 large loaf)
Preparation time: 20 min
Rising time: about 1 hr
Baking time: about 40 min
Oven temperature: 220°C, 425°F, Gas 7
Lowest rack in the oven
Suitable for freezing

50g (2oz) butter or margarine
150ml (¼pt) milk
50g (2oz) yeast
2 eggs, 1 × 5ml tsp (1tsp) salt
½ × 5ml tsp (½tsp) ground aniseed and fennel, mixed
2 onions, 1 clove garlic
about 100g (¼lb) cooked ham
125g (4¼oz) stone-ground wholewheat flour
300–400g (11–14oz) strong plain flour

1 Melt butter or margarine, add milk and keep the mixture lukewarm. Dissolve the yeast in a little of the mixture and add the remaining milk, together with the eggs, salt, aniseed, fennel and the stone-ground flour. Stir until well mixed.
2 Chop onions very finely and mix them with crushed garlic, the coarsely minced ham and about 150g (5oz) plain flour. Stir into the dough.
3 Knead the dough throughly and add more plain flour until it is elastic. Cover the dough and place in a warm place for about 40 min.
4 Remove the dough to a floured board and form a round loaf. Let the bread rise again for about 20 min, slash lightly in a diamond pattern and brush with water or milk. The bread can be sprinkled with 2–3 × 15ml tbsp (2–3tbsp) stone-ground flour, mixed with a little coarse sea-salt, aniseed and fennel. Bake for 40 min at 220°C, 425°F, Gas 7 and cool on a rack.

Yoghurt Bread

(makes 2 loaves)
Preparation time: 15 min
Rising time: about 1 hr
Baking time: about 30 min
Oven temperature: 200°C, 400°F, Gas 6
Lowest rack in the oven
Suitable for freezing

6 × 15ml tbsp (6tbsp) crushed whole wheat grains or 60g (2½oz) stone-ground wholewheat flour

½ litre (about 1pt) water
75g (3oz) yeast
1 × 15ml tbsp (1tbsp) salt
1 × 15ml tbsp (1tbsp) linseed (optional)
about 200ml (7fl oz) natural yoghurt
175g (6oz) wholemeal flour
about ¾kg (1lb 10oz) strong plain flour

1 Pour about 200ml (7fl oz) boiling water over the crushed wheat grains or the stone-ground wheat flour and let stand until lukewarm. Dissolve the yeast in the remaining water, also lukewarm, and add salt, the wheat grains, linseed and yoghurt; all at room temperature.
2 Stir in the wholemeal flour mixed with about half the plain flour. Combine thoroughly with a wooden spoon or mix for 3–4 min in a food mixer with a dough hook. Add more plain flour and work the dough with your hands until it is smooth and elastic. Cover and place in a warm place to rise for about 40 min.
3 Remove the dough from the bowl and place on a floured board. Knead it lightly, form two portions and let stand for 5 min. Pat or roll out until they are flat, fold over in the middle making an oval shape, and slash top (see illustration, page 18). Leave to rise again on a greased baking sheet for about 20 min.
4 Brush the loaves with water, milk or melted butter and sprinkle top with wheat grains or stone-ground wheat. Bake for 30 min at 200°C, 400°F, Gas 6 and cool on a wire rack.

Health Bread

(makes 1 loaf)
Preparation time: about 15 min
Rising time: about 1¼ hr
Baking time: 35–40 min
Oven temperature: 200°C, 400°F, Gas 6
Lowest rack in the oven
Suitable for freezing

50g (2g) yeast
200ml (7fl oz) lukewarm water
300ml (½pt) buttermilk
1 × 15ml tbsp (1tbsp) oil
100g (¼lb) wheat bran
2 × 5ml tsp (2tsp) salt
125g (4½oz) stone-ground wholewheat flour
about ½kg (1lb 2oz) strong plain flour

1 Dissolve the yeast in the lukewarm water and add lukewarm milk, oil, wheat bran, salt and wholewheat flour. Let the mixture stand for about 15 min.
2 Add plain flour, a little at a time, and knead the dough thoroughly. Cover and place in a warm place to rise for about 40 min.
3 Remove the dough and place on a floured board, knead it lightly and form into an oblong loaf. Put into a greased baking tin and set aside to rise in a warm place for about 20 min. Cut a slash lengthwise, brush with water and sprinkle a little wheat bran on top. Bake for 35–40 min at 200°C, 400°F, Gas 6 and cool the bread on a wire rack. For a soft crust, place a clean cloth over the bread while cooling.

Crusty Rolls

(makes 18–20 rolls)
Preparation time: about 20 min
Rising time: about ¾ hr
Baking time: about 15 min
Oven temperature: 220°C, 425°F, Gas 7
Middle rack in the oven
Suitable for freezing

½kg (1lb 2oz) strong plain flour
50g (2oz) yeast
400–500ml (¾–1pt) lukewarm milk
2 × 5ml tsp (2tsp) salt
½ × 5ml tsp (½tsp) sugar
1 egg for brushing
poppy or sesame seed

1 Sift the flour and put the crumbled yeast in a hollow in the middle. Dissolve the yeast, adding 100ml (4fl oz) lukewarm milk and add a little of the flour. Cover and leave in a warm place for about 15 min.
2 Add salt, sugar and lukewarm milk until the dough can be kneaded smooth and elastic, and let it stand for a further 15 min.
3 Remove the dough to a floured board, knead it and form 18–20 rolls. Leave these to rise again on a greased baking sheet for 15–20 min.
4 Brush the rolls with beaten egg and cut a slash in half of them with a thin, sharp knife. Sprinkle these rolls with poppy seed and the others with sesame seeds. Put a saucer or a pan with warm water in the bottom of the oven and bake the rolls for about 15 min at 220°C, 425°F, Gas 7. Cool on a wire rack.

Good Old-fashioned Breads

Spiced Bread

(makes 2 loaves)
Preparation time: 15–20 min
Rising time: 50–60 min
Baking time: about 30 min
Oven temperature: 200–220°C,
400–425°F, Gas 6–7
Lowest rack in the oven
Suitable for freezing

600g (1lb 5oz) strong plain flour
50g (2oz) yeast
300ml (½pt) lukewarm milk
50g (2oz) butter or margarine
2 eggs
2 × 5ml tsp (2tsp) salt
½ × 5ml tsp (½tsp) pepper
1 × 15ml tbsp (1tbsp) caraway seeds
1–2 × 5ml tsp (1–2tsp) coriander
  (optional)

1 Sift flour, salt and pepper and make a hollow in the centre. Put in the crumbled yeast, and the lukewarm milk and dissolve the yeast in the milk with a little of the flour. Cover and let stand for 15 min.
2 Add softened butter, 1 egg, ½ × 15ml tbsp (½tbsp) caraway seeds and ½ × 5ml tsp (½tsp) ground coriander. Knead the dough thoroughly. Cover and leave to rise in a warm place for around 20 min.
3 Remove dough to a floured board and divide it into two. Let the portions stand for 3–4 min, then shape into two oblong loaves. Let these rise again on a baking sheet for around 20 min.
4 Slash, brush with beaten egg and sprinkle remaining caraway seeds and coriander over the top. Bake as directed, then cool under a clean cloth on a wire rack.

Malt Bread

(makes 1 loaf)
Preparation time: about 15 min
Rising time: about 2 hr
Baking time: about 1 hr
Oven temperature: 200°C, 400°F, Gas 6
Lowest rack in the oven
Suitable for freezing

350g (¾lb) strong plain flour
350g (¾lb) rye flour

75g (3oz) sugar
1 × 5ml tsp (1tsp) salt
40g (1½oz) yeast
400ml (¾pt) lukewarm milk
100ml (4fl oz) malt beer
1 × 15ml tbsp (1tbsp) golden syrup
½ × 5ml tsp (½tsp) ground ginger
50g (2oz) raisins

1 Mix most of the flour with the sugar and salt. Dissolve the yeast in a little lukewarm milk and beer. Add to the flour together with the remaining liquid, mix to a dough and let it rise for ½–1 hr.
2 Mix in syrup and remaining flour mixed with the ginger and the raisins. Let the dough rise again for about ½ hr. Form into a round or oblong loaf, and let it rise on a baking sheet for about 15 min. Brush with sugared water and bake as directed.
This is an especially heavy and sweet dough, and therefore is made first as an ordinary dough without syrup. When the fermentation is well under way, the syrup is added together with the rest of the flour. Very sweet, heavy doughs should be made in this way.

French Country Bread

(makes 2 loaves)
Preparation time: about 20 min
Rising time: about 3 hr
Baking time: about 40 min
Oven temperature: 240 and 160°C, 475 and 325°F, Gas 9 and 3
Lowest rack in the oven
Suitable for freezing

25g (1oz) yeast
600ml (about 1pt) lukewarm water
1 × 15ml tbsp (1tbsp) salt
2 × 15ml tbsp (2tbsp) oil
about 1kg (about 2¼lb) strong plain flour

1 Dissolve the yeast in the lukewarm water. Add oil, salt and at least half the flour. Mix the dough thoroughly with a wooden spoon and knead in the rest of the plain flour with the hands. Cover the dough and place in a warm place to rise for about 2 hr at room temperature.
2 Remove the dough to a floured board and knead it lightly. Divide into two and let the portions stand for about 5 min. Roll out as two oblong loaves, cover them and place

on a baking sheet to rise again for about 1 hr.
3 Cut diagonal slashes, brush with water and sprinkle a little flour on top. Bake for 15–20 min at 240°C, 475°F, Gas 9, then reduce the heat to 160°C, 325°F, Gas 3 and bake for the remainder of the baking time. Place the loaves on a wire rack to cool.

Rolls with Herb Flavouring

(makes 25 rolls)
Preparation time: about 20 min
Rising time: about 50 min
Baking time: about 12–15 min
Oven temperature: 220–230°C, 425–450°F, Gas 7–8
Middle rack in the oven
Suitable for freezing

25g (1oz) yeast
250ml (9fl oz) lukewarm milk
about ½kg (1lb 2oz) strong plain flour
50g (2oz) butter or margarine
2 eggs
2 × 5ml tsp (2tsp) salt
½ × 5ml tsp (½tsp) nutmeg
4 × 15ml tbsp (4tbsp) chopped fresh herbs

1 Dissolve the yeast in about 100ml (4fl oz) lukewarm milk, stir in half the flour and set the dough aside to rise for 15 min.
2 Add softened butter, 1 egg, salt, the remaining milk, nutmeg and the chopped fresh herbs (chives, dillweed, parsley etc). Knead the rest of the flour into the dough until it is elastic. Place in a warm place to rise for about 20 min.
3 Remove the dough to a floured board and cut it into small portions to make rolls. Roll them out and let them rise again on a greased sheet for 15–20 min.
4 Cut a slit in each small roll with a sharp knife, brush with beaten egg and bake as directed. Place the rolls on a wire rack to cool.

In the basket and on the table are delicious Rolls with Herb Flavouring. On the table is tasty Spiced Bread sprinkled with caraway seeds and coriander.

Bread made with Sourdough

The baking of this type of bread must be planned well in advance, as the dough needs time to develop. But it needs very little attention and is no more difficult to work with than other types of yeast dough. The advantage is that the loaves are moist and keep well.

Coarse Rye Bread with Sourdough (see plate, page 6)
(makes 2 loaves)
Preparation time: about 20 min
Rising time: about 3 hr +
24 hr for the sourdough
Baking time: about 1 hr
Oven temperature: 200°C, 400°F, Gas 6
Lowest rack in the oven
Suitable for freezing

Sourdough : 50g (2oz) whole or crushed rye grains
100ml (4fl oz) water
200g (7oz) coarsely ground rye
300ml (½pt) buttermilk
Dough : 75g (3oz) yeast
300ml (½pt) lukewarm water
1 × 15ml tbsp (1tbsp) salt
650g (about 1lb 7oz) finely ground rye flour
300g (11oz) strong plain flour

1 Pour 100ml (4fl oz) boiling water over whole or crushed rye grains and let stand until the water is lukewarm. Add coarse rye flour and buttermilk and let the sourdough stand, covered, at room temperature for 24 hr.

2 Dissolve the yeast in the lukewarm water and stir in the sourdough. Add salt and finely ground rye flour and work the dough thoroughly. Knead in the plain flour until the dough is firm and smooth. Set it aside to rise at room temperature for about 2 hr.

3 Knead the dough well and divide it into two. Form loaves and place them in greased baking tins. Let them rise for 1 hr and brush them with water. Make a cut lengthwise and prick with a fork. Sprinkle whole rye grains on top and bake as directed. Place the loaves, covered, on a wire rack to cool. Wait a day before you slice the bread.

Rye Bread with Cottage Cheese and Sourdough
(makes 1 loaf)
Preparation time: about 20 min
Rising time: about 1¼ hr +
24 hr for sourdough
Baking time: about 40–45 min
Oven temperature: 200°C
400°F, Gas 6
Lowest rack in the oven
Suitable for freezing

Sourdough : 100g (4oz) coarsely ground rye flour
200g (7oz) cottage cheese
Dough : 50g (2oz) yeast
300ml (½pt) lukewarm water
200g (7oz) rye flour
3 × 5ml tsp (3tsp) salt
about 400g (11oz) strong plain flour

1 Stir together the coarse rye flour and the cottage cheese, cover and set aside for 24 hr at room tem-

Below : Two good breads made with sourdough, and which keep well – Rye Bread with Cottage Cheese, and Graham Bread.

perature or a little cooler (not in the refrigerator).

2 Stir the sourdough and yeast in the lukewarm water and add rye flour, salt, and most of the plain flour. Mix the dough thoroughly with the remaining plain flour, as needed. Let it stand to rise in a warm place for 45 min.

3 Knead the dough, form it into a round loaf and let it rise again for 30 min on a baking sheet.

4 Cut slashes or prick with a fork, brush with water and sprinkle a little flour on top. Bake as directed and cool on a wire rack.

Graham Bread with Sourdough
(makes 1 loaf)
Preparation time: 15–20 min
Rising time: about 1½ hr +24 hr for sourdough
Baking time: about 35–40 min
Oven temperature 200°C, 400°F, Gas 6
Lowest rack in the oven
Suitable for freezing

Sourdough: 300ml (½pt) buttermilk
200g (7oz) wholemeal flour
Dough: 50g (2oz) yeast
200ml (7fl oz) lukewarm water
2–3 × 5ml tsp (2–3tsp) salt
1 × 15ml tbsp (1tbsp) oil
200g (7oz) wholemeal flour
about 300g (11oz) strong plain flour

1 Stir the flour and buttermilk together to make the sourdough, cover and let stand at room temperature for 24 hr.

2 Dissolve the sourdough in the lukewarm water together with the yeast and add salt, oil and then the wholemeal flour. Work the dough thoroughly and knead in the plain flour. Cover and set aside to rise for about 1 hr.

3 Knead the dough on a floured board and form it into a large loaf. Set aside to rise on a baking sheet for about 30 min. Cut diagonal slashes, brush with water, and sprinkle a little flour on top. Bake as directed and leave the bread, covered, on a wire rack to cool.

Rye Bread with Sourdough
(makes 2 loaves)
Preparation time: about 15–20 min
Rising time: about 1½ hr + 48 hr for the sourdough
Baking time: about 1¼ hr

Oven temperature: 200°C, 400°F, Gas 6
Lowest rack in the oven
Suitable for freezing

Sourdough: 100g (¼lb) rye flour
100ml (4fl oz) buttermilk
½ × 5ml tsp (½tsp) salt
Dough: 50g (2oz) yeast
½ litre (about 1pt) lukewarm water
3 × 5ml tsp (3tsp) salt
½kg (1lb 2oz) rye flour
about 300g (11oz) strong plain flour

1 Mix together the 100g (¼lb) rye flour, buttermilk and salt, cover and set aside at room temperature for 48 hr.

2 Dissolve the sourdough in the lukewarm water together with the crumbled yeast. Add salt and rye flour, mix dough well and knead it, with the plain flour, until elastic. Cover and put in a warm place to rise for about 1 hr.

3 Knead the dough on a floured board and divide it into two. Form oblong loaves. Put them beside each other, with greased tinfoil between, in a small roasting pan or fireproof dish. Let them rise again for about 30 min.

4 Brush with water, prick with a fork and bake as directed.

Turn the loaves out onto a wire rack and cool a little before you separate them. Cover with a cloth. Wait 24 hr before you slice the bread.

Below: Rye Bread with Sourdough
is good with salami.

Wholesome Breads

Dark Country Bread

(makes 2 loaves)
Preparation time: about 15–20 min
Rising time: about 2 hr
Baking time: about 40 min
Oven temperature: about 200°C,
400°F, Gas 6
Lowest rack in the oven
Suitable for freezing

25g (1oz) yeast
½ litre (about 1pt) lukewarm water
3 × 5ml tsp (3tsp) salt
3 × 15ml tbsp (3tbsp) oil
180g (6½oz) rye flour
250g (9oz) wholemeal flour
about 400g (14oz) strong plain flour

1 Dissolve the yeast in the luke-warm water and add salt, oil, rye flour and wholemeal flour. Mix the dough smoothly until elastic and add plain flour until the dough is sufficiently firm. Cover and let stand in a warm place to rise for about 1½ hr.
2 Remove the dough to a floured board and divide it into two. Form into two oblong loaves and put them on a baking sheet to rise for about 30 min. Brush with water, prick well with a fork or slash. Let the loaves cool on a wire rack with, if you want a soft crust, a cloth on top.

VARIATION
For a coarser bread, use coarsely ground rye flour instead of ordinary rye flour.

Rye Bread

(makes 2 loaves)
Preparation time: about 15–20 min
Rising time: about 1 hr 20–25 min
Baking time: about 35–40 min
Oven temperature: 200°C, 400°F,
Gas 6
Lowest rack in the oven
Suitable for freezing

50g (2oz) yeast
200ml (7fl oz) lukewarm water
1 × 15ml tbsp (1tbsp) salt
400ml (¾pt) buttermilk
3 × 15ml tbsp (3tbsp) oil
400g (14oz) rye flour
about ½kg (1lb 2oz) strong plain flour

1 Dissolve the yeast in the luke-warm water and add salt, buttermilk (at room temperature), oil and rye flour. Mix the dough thoroughly and add plain flour. Cover, and set aside in a warm place to rise for about 1 hr.
2 Knead the dough lightly and divide into two. Form round or oblong loaves, cover and place on a baking sheet for 20–25 min to rise again. Brush the loaves with milk, cream or beaten egg. Cut diagonal slashes on oblong loaves and a diamond pattern, with 2–3cm (¾–1in) spaces, on round loaves (see page 16). Bake as directed and cool on a wire rack.

VARIATION
Rye bread can be baked with equal parts of rye flour and strong plain flour if you want a firmer bread. If 1–2 × 15ml tbsp (1–2tbsp) caraway seeds are added, the bread will have an interesting flavour.

Basket Bread

(makes 2 loaves)
Preparation time: about 20 min
Rising time: about 1 hr
Baking time: about 30 min
Oven temperature: 200°C, 400°F,
Gas 6
Lowest rack in the oven
Suitable for freezing

50g (2oz) yeast
400ml (¾pt) lukewarm water
3 × 5ml tsp (3tsp) salt
about 200ml (7fl oz) natural yoghurt
250g (9oz) wholemeal flour
300g (11oz) rye flour
about 300g (11oz) strong plain flour

1 Dissolve the yeast in the luke-warm water and add the yoghurt, which should be at room temperature. Add salt, rye flour and wholemeal flour, and mix thoroughly with a wooden spoon or a fork until elastic. Knead in the plain flour and put the dough, covered, in a warm place to rise for 30–40 min.
2 Knead the dough on a floured board and divide it into two. Form into round loaves and put them into greased and flour-sprinkled baskets. Cover, and leave to rise again for about 30 min.
3 Turn the loaves out carefully onto a baking sheet and bake as directed. Brush the baked loaves with luke-warm water, sprinkle with a little flour, and put on a wire rack to cool.

Bread Baked in a Tin or Mould

Herb Bread (left)
(makes 2 loaves)
Mould: clay flower-pots
Preparation time: about 25 min
Rising time: about 50 min
Baking time: about 40 min
Oven temperature: 220°C, 425°F,
Gas 7
Lowest rack in the oven
Suitable for freezing

½kg (1lb 2oz) strong plain flour
50g (2oz) yeast
150ml (¼pt) lukewarm milk
2 × 5ml tsp (2tsp) salt
½ × 5ml tsp (½tsp) sugar
50g (2oz) butter or margarine
2 eggs
4 × 15ml tbsp (4tbsp) chopped
*   dillweed*
1–2 × 5ml tsp (1–2tsp) dried fennel
½ × 5ml tsp (½tsp) dried rosemary
pinch of nutmeg
1–2 × 5ml tsp (1–2tsp) aniseed

1 Sift the flour and make a hollow in the centre. Put in the crumbled yeast, pour lukewarm milk (at about 37°C, 100°F) over it and dissolve the yeast with salt, sugar and a little of the flour. Cover the bowl and leave in a warm place for 15 min for the dough to rise.
2 Stir melted, slightly cooled butter with the lightly beaten egg, finely chopped dillweed, herbs and nutmeg. Keep a little of the aniseed for decoration.
3 Pour the mixture into the bowl with the dough and mix thoroughly. Cover and set aside in a warm place for about 15 min to rise.
4 Remove the dough to a floured board, divide it into two and put into flower-pots which have been washed, dried and brushed with oil. Put in large polythene bags and set aside to rise for about 20 min. Brush with water and sprinkle the rest of the aniseed on top. Bake at 220°C, 425°F, Gas 7 for about 40 min. Turn the loaves out carefully onto a wire rack to cool. They can be put back into the flower-pots when they are to be served.
Herb bread can be frozen with or without the flower-pots, but clay flower-pots easily break if jolted in the freezer. They must therefore be well protected and should be wrapped in tinfoil.

White Tin-loaf (above)
(makes 2 loaves)
2 × 1kg (2lb) loaf tins
Preparation time: about 15–20 min
Rising time: about 50 min
Baking time: about 30–40 min
Oven temperature: 220°C, 425°F, Gas 7
Lowest rack in the oven
Suitable for freezing

50g (2oz) butter or margarine
600ml (about 1pt) skimmed milk
50g (2oz) yeast
½ × 15ml tbsp (½tbsp) salt
½–1 × 5ml tsp (½–1tsp) sugar
about 1kg (2¼lb) strong plain flour
egg or cream for brushing

1 Melt butter or margarine and add the milk, making sure that the mixture does not get warmer than 37°C (100°F). Dissolve the yeast in about 100ml (4fl oz) of this liquid and add salt and sugar.
2 Stir in the remaining liquid alternately with at least half the flour, and mix the dough thoroughly with a wooden spoon or for 3–4 min in a food mixer with a dough hook. Knead in the rest of the flour with your hands, cover and put in a warm place to rise for about 30 min.
3 Remove the dough to a floured board and divide it into two. Shape into two large 'buns' and let them stand 4–5 min. Roll out or flatten the 'buns' into thick slabs, fold the sides in towards the middle and fold them again lengthwise into oblong loaves. Put them into greased tins. Brush with egg or cream.
4 Bake the loaves at 220°C, 425°F, Gas 7 for 30–40 min. Take them out of the tins for the last 10 min if the bottom and sides are not brown enough. Place them on their side and turn them after 5 min. Cool on a wire rack. You can also make French Bread from this recipe. Roll out two long portions, score 3–4 times diagonally with a sharp knife, brush with cream or egg and bake for about 30 min at 200°C, 400°F, Gas 6.

Additions to Vary the Flavour

Bread may be varied to suit your taste and the occasion. The following recipes use a neutral basic recipe as a starting point and add spices, onion, cheese, tomatoes, mushrooms, bacon, olives and salami. You will find them interesting to bake as well as to eat.

Basic Dough

(makes 2–4 loaves depending on size)
Preparation time: about 20 min
Rising time: about 1 hr
Baking time: 35–45 min
Oven temperature: 200–220°C, 400–425°F, Gas 6–7
Lowest rack in the oven
Suitable for freezing

50g (2oz) yeast
about 700ml (1¼pt) lukewarm water
2–3 × 5ml tsp (2–3tsp) salt
250g (9oz) rye flour
about 750g (1lb 10oz) strong plain flour

Dissolve the crumbled yeast in 100–200 ml (4–7fl oz) lukewarm water. Add salt, the remaining water, the rye flour and half of the plain flour. Stir the dough thoroughly and knead in the rest of the plain flour with the hands until elastic. Cover and put in a warm place to rise for about 30 min.
2 Remove the dough to a floured board and knead it slightly. Add the flavour ingredients (see individual recipes). Divide the dough, form into loaves and set aside to rise again for 30 min. Bake according to recipes.

Onion Bread (left)

(makes 2 loaves)
Preparation time, Rising time and Baking time: see Basic Dough

½ quantity Basic Dough
3–4 onions
½ × 5ml tsp (½tsp) pepper
2 × 15ml tbsp (2tbsp) butter or margarine
cream for brushing top

1 Set aside the dough to rise, meanwhile clean and roughly chop the onions. Sauté them in butter on low heat for 5 min, then cool.

2 Knead the dough with the onion, pepper and a little more plain flour until it is elastic and does not stick to the board. Form two long thin loaves and set them to rise, covered, on a greased baking sheet for 25–30 min.

3 Cut diagonal slashes with a sharp knife, brush with cream and sprinkle a little flour on top. Bake for 30–35 min at 220°C, 425°F, Gas 7, and cool on a wire rack.

Serve Onion Bread cut in slices, with soup and other supper dishes. It is also good just with butter and for any kind of sandwich.

Cheese Bread (right)

(makes 1 loaf)

Preparation time, Rising time and Baking time: see Basic Dough (page 28)

½ quantity Basic Dough
150g (5oz) cheese
1 small onion
cream for brushing top

1 Set the dough to rise, meanwhile grate the cheese coarsely. Chop the onion finely.

2 Remove the dough to a floured board and knead in the cheese and onion together with a little more plain flour. Form the dough into a round loaf, put it on a greased baking sheet and let it rise again under a cloth or polythene for about 30 min.

3 Brush the bread with cream, sprinkle a thin layer of flour over the top and bake at 200°C, 400°F, Gas 6 for about 45 min. Place the bread on a rack to cool.

Cheese Bread is delicious with soups, casserole dishes, vegetable dishes and salads.

Pizza Bread

(makes 1 loaf)
1kg (2lb) loaf tin
Preparation time, Rising time and Baking time: see Basic Dough (page 28)

½ quantity Basic Dough
2 × 15ml tbsp (2tbsp) butter or margarine, 1 onion
200g (7oz) raw minced meat
10 stuffed olives (optional)
3 small tomatoes
salt, pepper and paprika
marjoram, oregano and basil

1 Set the dough aside to rise.
2 Brown the finely chopped onion and the minced meat lightly in the butter and add the chopped stuffed olives. Scald and skin the tomatoes, cut them into four and squeeze out the seeds. Roughly chop the tomato flesh and put into the saucepan together with the onion and the minced meat.
3 Cook the mixture until all liquid has evaporated. Season with the fresh or dried herbs and spices.
4 Roll out the dough fairly thinly but with one side equal in length to a 1kg (2lb) loaf tin. Spread the filling on the dough, moisten the edges with water and roll up like a Swiss roll. Place in a greased tin, cover and let stand for about 20 min to rise. Brush top with water, sprinkle a thin layer of flour over and bake for about 45 min at 200°C, 400°F, Gas 6. Put on a wire rack to cool.

Bacon Bread

(makes 1 loaf)
Preparation time, Rising time and Baking time: see Basic Dough (page 28)

½ quantity Basic Dough
100g (¼lb) lean bacon
1 leek, 1 small onion
100g (¼lb) mushrooms, dill
1 × 15ml tbsp (1tbsp) chopped chives
1 × 15ml tbsp (1tbsp) chopped parsley
salt, whole peppercorns
coriander seeds

1 Set the dough aside to rise.
2 Meanwhile, roughly chop the bacon and brown the pieces lightly in a dry frying pan, together with the finely sliced leek, chopped onion and chopped mushrooms.

3 Drain off the bacon fat, mix the finely chopped herbs with the vegetables and bacon and season to taste. Knead the filling into the dough, possibly with a little more flour.
4 Divide the dough into three portions. Roll each out to a long, thin roll about 40 cm (16 in) long and plait them together. Fold the ends under. Leave to rise again on the baking sheet for about 20 min, brush with water and sprinkle with a little whole or crushed peppercorns and coriander seeds.
Bake for about 45 min at 200°C, 400°F, Gas 6. Place the bread on a wire rack to cool.

Salami Bread

(makes 1 loaf)
Preparation time, Rising time and Baking time: see Basic Dough (page 28)

½ quantity Basic Dough
4 onions, 150–200g (5–7oz) salami
50–75g (2–3oz) cheese
2 × 15ml tbsp (2tbsp) finely chopped parsley, coarse sea-salt

1 Put the dough aside to rise. Cut onions, salami and cheese into small cubes and knead them into the dough together with the parsley and possibly a little more flour, add seasoning to taste.
2 Form the dough into a round, rather flat loaf and put it aside to rise again on a greased baking sheet. Cut a diamond pattern as shown on page 16, brush with water and sprinkle sea-salt mixed with 1 × 15ml tbsp (1tbsp) plain flour on top.
3 Bake for about 45 min at 200°C, 400°F, Gas 6 and put the bread to cool on a wire rack.

Other Suggestions

Don't just rely on the recipes already given for adding different ingredients. Be adventurous and think up other combinations to give an interesting taste. Experiment with celery, colourful red and green peppers or add all kinds of sausages and sausagemeat to the same basic dough. There are so many other kinds of herbs and spices to try too.

From left to right: Bacon Bread with bacon, leek, onion and mushrooms; Salami Bread with onion and cheese; Pizza Bread.

Exciting Breads

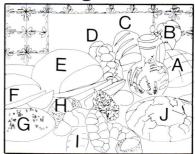

A Linseed Bread (p 16), B and D plaited breads, C Onion Bread (p 28), E Cheese Bread (p 29), F Graham Bread (p 10), G Coriander Bread (below), H Crusty Rolls (p 19), I Plaited Rolls (p 34), J Rye Bread (p 25).

Coriander Bread

(makes 5–6 loaves)
Preparation time: about 20 min
Rising time: about 45 min
Baking time: about 20 min
Oven temperature: 220°C, 425°F, Gas 7
Middle rack in the oven
Suitable for freezing

50g (2oz) yeast, 250ml (9fl oz)
  lukewarm skimmed milk
2 × 5ml tsp (2tsp) salt
½ × 5ml tsp (½tsp) honey
1 egg
1 × 15ml tbsp (1tbsp) coriander
1 × 15ml tbsp (1tbsp) linseed
½ × 5ml tsp (½tsp) aniseed
250g (9oz) rye flour
about 350g (¾lb) strong plain flour

1 Dissolve the yeast in the lukewarm milk and add salt, honey, egg and a coarsely ground mixture of coriander, linseed and aniseed. Stir in the rye flour until the dough is elastic. Then knead in the plain flour with your hands.

2 Let the dough rise in a warm place, covered, for about 30 min. Remove to a floured board and divide into five or six portions. Form these into 'buns' and roll them flat. Let them rise again for about 15 min on a baking sheet.

3 Brush the loaves with water and sprinkle whole or crushed coriander seeds and a little flour on top. Bake for 20 min at 220°C, 425°F, Gas 7 and cool on a wire rack. Coriander Bread is excellent with soups and other supper dishes.

Dinner Rolls

Small rolls are a welcome addition to a dinner party. It is easy and cheap to make these rolls yourself, and when you have once tried you will certainly want to do it more often. As with most yeast baking, small rolls are well suited for freezing, so it is worth while baking a large quantity when you are about it.

Dinner Rolls with Cottage Cheese

(makes 60–80 small rolls)
Preparation time: about 30 min
Rising time: about 30–40 min
Baking time: about 12–15 min
Oven temperature: 220°C, 425°F, Gas 7
Middle rack in the oven
Suitable for freezing

50g (2oz) butter or margarine
500ml (about 1pt) skimmed milk
225g (8oz) cottage cheese
50g (2oz) yeast
1½–2 × 5ml tsp (1½–2tsp) salt
about 1kg (2¼lb) strong plain flour
1 egg for brushing top
Decoration: whole wheat grains, sesame seeds, poppy seeds, sea-salt or the equivalent

1 Melt the butter or margarine, add the milk and keep the mixture at under 37°C (100°F). Crumble the yeast and dissolve it in 100–200ml (4–7fl oz) of the liquid. Add the remaining milk, the cottage cheese and the salt. Stir in half the flour, mixing in thoroughly.
2 Remove the dough to a floured board, add the remaining flour a little at a time and knead well. Flatten or roll out the dough and fold it together again. Repeat this several times. Put in a bowl, sprinkle a thin layer of flour over, cover and put in a warm place. The dough will have finished rising when it has about doubled in size.
3 Remove to a floured board, divide it into four portions and roll each of them out to a long 'sausage'. Divide each into 15–20 pieces and shape

Plaited Rolls

1 Form 14–16 rounds from ¼ quantity Basic Dough (see page 28) and divide each round into three.
2 Roll out into thin 'sausages' and press together, three at one end.
3 Plait as shown and turn under the ends. Leave to rise again on a greased baking sheet for about 15 min.
4 Brush with egg and decorate. Bake as directed for Basic Dough.

1
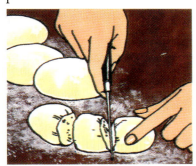

2

3
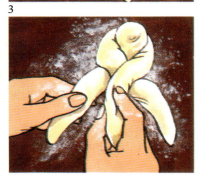

4

into small round or oval rolls, mini loaves or plaited bread. (See diagrams below for making Plaited Rolls).

4 Leave to rise again on a greased baking sheet for 15–20 min. Make a cut in the round or oval rolls with a sharp knife, or clip a notch with sharp scissors.

5 Brush rolls or loaves with beaten egg and, if liked, sprinkle seeds or sea-salt on top. Bake until they are golden in colour and cool them on a wire rack.

To freeze, pack them in tinfoil before they are completely cool. Let them stand in the freezer wrappings until they are quite cold and then put them in the freezer. To thaw, heat them in the oven at 190–200°C, 375–400°F, Gas 5–6 for a few minutes.

Croissants (Cresent Rolls)

1 Roll out the dough to a square on a floured board.

2 Fold the dough in over the butter and roll out carefully.

3 Fold together, turn a quarter of the way round and roll out again. Repeat this three times.

4 Dip a knife in flour and cut each of the two round slabs into eight triangles.

5 Begin from the outside of the triangle and roll towards the tip. If you are afraid that the roll will come undone, you can brush the tip with a little water or egg. Bend into crescents, place them on a greased baking sheet to rise again, brush with beaten egg and bake as explained in the recipe.

Croissants (Crescent Rolls)
(makes 16 croissants)
Preparation time: about 30 min
Rising time: about 5½ hr
Baking time: about 15–20 min
Oven temperature: 220°C, 425°F, Gas 7
Middle rack in the oven
Suitable for freezing

25g (1oz) yeast
250ml (9fl oz) lukewarm milk
½–1 × 5ml tsp (½–1tsp) salt
200g (7oz) butter or margarine
about ½kg (1lb 2oz) strong plain flour
1 egg for brushing top

1 Crumble the yeast and dissolve it in the lukewarm milk. Mix to an elastic smooth dough with the salt and 200g (7fl oz) flour. Crumble 100g (¼lb) butter in about 200g (7oz) plain flour with the tips of the fingers. Sprinkle the butter and flour mixture into the yeast dough, and mix thoroughly with a wooden spoon. More flour can be added to make the dough smooth.

2 Cover and set the dough to rise in a cool place for 4–5 hr or overnight.

3 Remove dough to a floured board, knead it well and roll it out to a square. Roll 100g (¼lb) chilled butter between two layers of plastic, remove the plastic and lay the butter in the middle of the dough. Fold the dough and roll it out until you can see the butter. Fold the dough together as shown in the illustration.

4 Let the crescents rise again on a greased baking sheet, then bake for 15–20 min at 220°C, 425°F, Gas 7. Cool on a wire rack.

1

2

3

4

5

One Dough – Many Loaves

There are many ways of shaping yeast dough. Here are a few examples, all baked with the same basic dough except for the genuine French bread.

Basic Dough
Preparation time: about 15 min
Rising time: 1 hr altogether
Baking time: about 30 min
Oven temperature: 200–220°C, 400–425°F, Gas 6–7
Lowest rack in the oven
Suitable for freezing

50g (2oz) yeast
100ml (4fl oz) lukewarm water
250ml (9fl oz) skimmed milk
1 × 15ml tbsp (1tbsp) salt
2 × 15ml tbsp (2tbsp) oil
175g (6oz) rye flour
about 400g (15oz) strong plain flour

1 Dissolve the yeast in the lukewarm water and add lukewarm milk, salt, oil, rye flour and most of the plain flour.
2 Mix the dough thoroughly and knead in the remaining plain flour with the hands until the dough is elastic, even and not too hard. Cover and put in a warm place to rise for about 35–40 min, until doubled in bulk.
3 Shape the dough and allow to rise again as explained in the individual recipes, and bake as directed above.

Twisted Bread
(makes 1–2 loaves)

1 Remove the basic dough to a floured board and knead it lightly. Form into one large or two small, oblong loaves and twist them a couple of times.
2 Cover and let them rise again on a baking sheet for 20–25 min. Make a cut lengthwise with a sharp knife and brush them with water. Bake according to the basic recipe and cool on a wire rack.

Round Wheat Bread
(makes 1 loaf)

1 Knead the basic dough lightly on a floured board after it has risen and form a large round loaf. Let this rise on a baking sheet for 20–25 min under a cloth.

2 Cut a diamond pattern with a sharp knife, brush with water or milk, and bake according to the basic recipe. Cool the loaf on a wire rack.

Wreaths
(makes 1–2 wreaths)

1 Knead the basic dough lightly on a floured board after it has finished rising. Roll out into two or four long 'sausages'. Twine these into one or two wreaths.

2 Let the wreaths rise again on a baking sheet for 20–25 min. Brush with water or milk. Bake thin wreaths for 20 min at 220–230°C, 425–450°F, Gas 7–8 and a thick wreath for 30–35 min at 200°C, 400°F, Gas 6. Cool on a wire rack. Sprinkle the wreaths with poppy or sesame seeds before baking.

Sesame Star
(makes 1 star)

1 Knead the risen dough lightly on a floured board. Make a large 'bun' of about a fourth of the dough, and place it in the middle of a greased baking sheet. Divide the rest of the dough into six and form small round shapes, a little pointed at one end. Place them closely around the large 'bun' with the points facing outward.

2 Let the star rise again for 20–25 min, covered. Make cuts to emphasise the star form (see illustration). Brush with milk, sprinkle sesame seeds on top and bake according to the basic recipe.

Crescents with Poppy Seeds
(see plate, page 6)
(makes 16–24 crescents)

1 When the dough has finished rising, remove it to a floured board and knead it lightly. Roll out into two round slabs and cut each slab into 8–10 triangles. Roll them up, starting at the broad end and bending them a little.

2 Place the crescents, with the point down, on a greased baking sheet and let them rise again under a cloth for about 20 min. Brush with cream or beaten egg and sprinkle poppy seeds on top.
Bake for about 15 min at 220–230°C, 425–450°F, Gas 7–8 and cool on a wire rack.

French Bread (Baguette)
(makes 3–4 loaves)
Preparation time: about 15–20 min
Rising time: about 2½ hr
Baking time: about 12–15 min
Oven temperature: 240–260°C, 475–500°F, Gas 9
Middle rack in the oven
Suitable for freezing

25g (1oz) yeast
300ml (½pt) lukewarm water
2–3 × 5ml tsp (2–3tsp) salt
1 × 15ml tbsp (1tbsp) oil
about ½kg (1lb 2oz) strong plain flour

1 Dissolve the crumbled yeast in lukewarm water and add salt, oil and most of the flour. Mix thoroughly and knead in the remaining flour until the dough is elastic. Cover and place in a warm spot to rise for about 2 hr.

2 Remove to a floured board, divide into three pieces and form each piece into a ball. Let the balls stand for 4–5 min before rolling them out into long, thin 'sausages'. Stop for a few minutes if the dough begins to contract.

3 Cover with a cloth and set aside to rise again on a greased baking sheet for 20–30 min. Brush with lightly salted lukewarm water and make two or three long S-shaped cuts with a razor blade.

4 Place a little heatproof bowl containing lukewarm water in the bottom of the pre-heated oven and bake the loaves for 12–15 min at 240–265°C, 475–500°F, Gas 9. If you want an extra crisp crust, brush with water during the baking. Place the loaves to cool on a wire rack.

TIP
Burned Crust
If the loaves seem to be getting too brown on top, put a piece of paper over them so that they do not get burned before they have finished baking.

50g (2oz) yeast
350ml (12fl oz) milk
2 × 15ml tbsp (2tbsp) oil
2 × 5ml tsp (2tsp) salt
1 × 5ml tsp (1tsp) sugar
about ½kg (1lb 2oz) strong plain
    flour

1 Dissolve the yeast in lukewarm milk and add oil, salt, sugar and most of the flour. Mix the dough thoroughly until it is smooth, and knead in the rest of the flour. Cover and set aside in a warm place to rise for about 30 min.

2 Remove the dough to a floured board and divide it into two. Roll one part out to a slab about 1cm (½in) thick. Punch out rounds about 8cm (3in) in diameter with a glass, and let them rise again for about 20 min on a greased baking sheet, covered with a cloth or polythene.

3 Collect the pieces of dough that are left over, knead them with the other half of the dough and roll out finger-thick 'sausages' about 10cm (4in) long. Cover and leave to rise again for about 20 min on a greased baking sheet. Brush with water or milk and bake for 15 min at 200°C, 400°F, Gas 6. Cool on a wire rack.

Walnut Bread

(makes 2 loaves)
Preparation time: about 20 min
Rising time: about 1¼ hr
Baking time: about 30 min
Oven temperature: 200–220°C, 400–425°F, Gas 6–7
Lowest rack in the oven
Suitable for freezing

2 × 15ml tbsp (2tbsp) butter or
    margarine, 250ml (9fl oz) water
50g (2oz) yeast
350ml (12fl oz) buttermilk
3 × 5ml tsp (3tsp) salt
100g (¼lb) stone-ground wholewheat
    flour
75–100g (3–4oz) walnuts
about ½kg (1lb 2oz) strong plain
    flour

1 Melt the butter, add the water, and warm slightly. Dissolve the yeast in the mixture and add luke-warm milk, salt and wholewheat flour. Chop the walnuts finely and stir them into the dough together with most of the plain flour. Mix the dough thoroughly and add more plain flour until the dough is smooth

Cheap but Wholesome

Viennese Rolls, Hamburger Rolls

(makes about 24 rolls)
Preparation time: about 20 min
Rising time: about 50 min
Baking time: about 15 min
Oven temperature: 200°C, 400°F, Gas 6
Middle rack in the oven
Suitable for freezing

but not too firm. Cover and set aside to rise in a warm place for 45–50 min. Knead the dough a little after it has risen for about 20 min.

2 Remove the dough to a floured board, form it into two balls, then shape these into ovals. Let these rise for 20–25 min, covered, on a greased baking sheet.

3 Brush the loaves with water or milk. Cut a star pattern with a sharp knife and bake them for about 30 min at 200–220°C, 400–425°F, Gas 6–7. Cool on a wire rack.

Saffron or Caraway Kringels
(make about 20 kringels)
Preparation time: about 20–25 min
Rising time: about 1 hr
Baking time: about 15 min
Oven temperature: 220°C, 425°F, Gas 7
Middle rack in the oven
Suitable for freezing

100g ($\frac{1}{4}$lb) butter or margarine
350ml (12fl oz) milk
25g (1oz) yeast
1 × 5ml tsp (1tsp) salt
1 × 5ml tsp (1tsp) sugar, 2 eggs
about $\frac{1}{2}$kg (1lb 2oz) strong plain flour
$\frac{1}{4}$ × 5ml tsp ($\frac{1}{4}$tsp) saffron
$\frac{1}{2}$–1 × 15ml tbsp ($\frac{1}{2}$–1tbsp) caraway seeds

1 Melt the butter and add the milk. Dissolve the yeast in the tepid mixture and add salt, sugar and 1 egg. If making saffron kringels, add the saffron; for caraway kringels add half the caraway seeds.

2 Stir in half the flour and knead in the rest with the hands until the dough is smooth and not too firm. Cover and set aside in a warm place to rise for 35–40 min.

3 Remove the dough to a floured board and divide it in 20 portions which should be left to rest for about 5 min. Roll out to long, thin 'sausages' and shape into rings or figure eights. Cover, and leave to rise on a greased baking sheet for about 20 min. Brush with beaten egg and sprinkle the caraway kringels with the remaining caraway seeds. Bake for 15 min at 220°C, 425°F, Gas 7 and cool on a rack.

Rusks (right)
(makes about 50 rusks)
Preparation time: about 25 min

Rising time: about 1 hr
Baking time: about 12–15 min
Drying time: 1–2 hr
Oven temperature: 220 and 110°C, 425 and 225°F, Gas 7 and $\frac{1}{4}$
Middle rack in the oven

50g (2oz) yeast
250ml (9fl oz) milk
1 × 5ml tsp (1tsp) salt
3 × 15ml tbsp (3tbsp) sugar
1 egg, 75g (3oz) butter or margarine
about $\frac{1}{2}$kg (1lb 2oz) strong plain flour

1 Dissolve the yeast in lukewarm milk, add salt, sugar, egg and half the flour. Mix the dough until smooth with a wooden spoon, or use a food mixer with a dough hook for 3–4 min. Cover the dough and put in a warm place to rise for 20 min.

2 Rub the butter into the remaining flour, mix it with the dough which has finished rising and knead thoroughly. Let it rise for 15–20 min more.

3 Remove the dough to a floured board, divide and shape it into small rounds. Let these rise again on a greased baking sheet for 15–20 min, then bake for 12–15 min at 220°C, 425°F, Gas 7. Turn the thermostat down to 110°C, 225°F, Gas $\frac{1}{4}$.

4 Divide the buns into two with a fork and lay them on the baking sheet with the cut surface uppermost. Let them stay in the oven until they are dry right through and a nice golden colour.

Hard Rolls (white and brown)

(makes about 48 rolls)
Preparation time: about 25 min
Rising time: about 1 hr
Baking time: about 10 min
Drying time: 2–3 hr at 110°C,
225°F, Gas ¼ with the oven door ajar
Oven temperature: 230°C, 450°F,
Gas 8
Middle rack in the oven

White Rolls

50g (2oz) yeast, 500ml (about 1pt)
    milk, 1 × 5ml tsp (1tsp) salt
125g (4¼oz) butter or margarine
75g (3oz) sugar
about 900g (2lb) strong plain flour

Brown Rolls

50g (2oz) yeast, 500ml (about 1pt)
    milk, 1 × 5ml tsp (1tsp) salt
200g (7oz) butter or margarine
100g (¼lb) sugar
350g (¾lb) stone-ground wholewheat
    flour
½kg (1lb 2oz) strong plain flour

Wholewheat Rolls

100g (¼lb) yeast, 500ml (about 1pt)
    milk, 1 × 5ml tsp (1tsp) salt
200g (7oz) butter or margarine
2 × 15ml tbsp (2tbsp) sugar or
    golden syrup
about 1kg (2¼lb) stone-ground
    wholewheat flour

1 Dissolve the yeast in a little of the lukewarm milk.
2 Rub butter into flour and add salt and sugar or golden syrup. Add the yeast mixture and the rest of the lukewarm milk and work the dough until it is smooth and firm. Cover and set aside in a warm place for about 30 min to rise.
3 Remove the dough to a floured board and knead it thoroughly. Divide into about 48 portions (first into 6, then each of these into 8). Shape into round or oval buns. Cover with a cloth and put aside to rise on a greased baking sheet for about 30 min.
4 Bake for about 10 min at 230°C, 450°F, Gas 8 and cool on a wire rack. Turn the thermostat down to about 110°C, 225°F, Gas ¼.
5 Divide the buns with a fork and place them, cut side up, on the baking sheet. Dry them for 2–3 hr at the lower temperature with the oven door a little ajar. Several trays of rolls can be dried at the same time.

Wholewheat Buns

(makes 16–18 buns)
Preparation time: about 15–20 min
Rising time: about 1 hr
Baking time: about 20 min
Oven temperature: 200°C, 400°F,
Gas 6
Middle rack in the oven
Suitable for freezing

200ml (7fl oz) lukewarm water
1 × 15ml tbsp (1tbsp) butter
50g (2oz) yeast
200ml (7fl oz) buttermilk or natural
    yoghurt
1½–2 × 5ml tsp (1½–2tsp) salt
150g (5oz) stone-ground wholewheat
    flour
about 400g (14oz) strong plain flour

1 Dissolve the yeast in lukewarm water with the melted butter. Add lukewarm buttermilk or yoghurt, salt, wholewheat flour and most of the plain flour. Mix the dough thoroughly and add more plain flour until the dough is smooth. Cover and set aside in a warm place to rise for about 40 min.
2 Remove the dough to a floured board and form it into a long roll. Divide it, shape into buns, and place these on a baking sheet to rise again for about 20 min.
3 Brush the buns with water or milk and sprinkle a little coarsely ground wholewheat flour on top. Bake as directed, then cool on a wire rack.

Nut Buns

(makes 24 buns)
Preparation time: about 15–20 min
Rising time: about 50 min
Baking time: about 18–20 min
Oven temperature: 200–220°C,
400–425°F, Gas 6–7
Middle rack in the oven
Suitable for freezing

50g (2oz) yeast
500ml (about 1pt) lukewarm water
2 × 5ml tsp (2tsp) salt
1 × 5ml tsp (1tsp) sugar
1 × 15ml tbsp (1tbsp) oil
75g (3oz) nuts
200g (7oz) stone-ground wholewheat
    flour
400–500g (14–18oz) strong plain
    flour

1 Dissolve the yeast in lukewarm water and add salt, sugar, oil, chopped nuts, wholewheat flour and most of the plain flour. Mix thoroughly, adding more plain flour until the dough is smooth. Cover and put in a warm place to rise for 30–35 min.
2 Remove the dough to a floured board and form buns. Place these on a greased baking sheet to rise again, covered, for about 20 min. Brush with water, milk or melted butter, and sprinkle a little wholewheat flour or chopped nuts on top. Bake for 18–20 min at 200–220°C, 400–425°F, Gas 6–7 and cool on a wire rack.

Flat Breads

(makes about 32 pieces)
Preparation time: about 15 min
Rising time: about 45 min
Baking time: 12–15 min
Oven temperature: 200–220°C,
400–425°F, Gas 6–7
Middle rack in the oven
Store in airtight tins

50g (2oz) yeast
250ml (9fl oz) milk
150g (5oz) butter or margarine
    about 400g (14oz) strong plain
    flour
200g (7oz) wholemeal flour

1 Heat the milk until it is lukewarm. Melt the butter and cool. Dissolve the yeast in a little of the milk and add the rest of the milk and half the butter. Add most of the flour until the dough is firm. Knead well, cover, and put in a warm place to rise for about 30 min.
2 Work the rest of the butter into the dough and add more flour. Divide the dough into portions and form evenly shaped buns. Leave them to rise for about 15 min.
3 Roll out the buns into very thin, round 'pancakes', preferably with a diamond-patterned or fluted rolling-pin. Punch a little hole in the middle of each. Prick the surface with a fork and bake on a greased baking sheet at 220–220°C, 400–425°F, Gas 6–7 until a nice golden colour. Cool on a wire rack.

Oven Squares

(makes 24 pieces)
Preparation time: about 15 min
Rising time: about 30 min
Baking time: about 15 min
Oven temperature: 220°C, 425°F,
Gas 7
Middle rack in the oven
Suitable for freezing

Freshly baked Caraway Kringels are delicious with coffee or tea.

of chilled butter on two-thirds of the rolled out dough and fold and roll out as shown on page 49. Repeat the rolling out and folding 3–4 times.

3 When rolling out for the last time, the slab of dough should be oblong-shaped and folded into three, lengthwise. Cut 5–6cm (2–2½in) wide pieces and place on a greased baking sheet to rise for 30 min. Brush with egg, sprinkle with poppy seeds and bake for 12–15 min at 220°C, 425°F, Gas 7. Cool on a wire rack.

Batch Buns

(makes 8 buns)
Preparation time: about 20 min
Rising time: about 1 hr
Baking time: about 15–20 min
Second baking time: 10–12 min
Oven temperature: 220 and 240°C, 425 and 475°F, Gas 7–9
Middle rack in the oven
Suitable for freezing

50g (2oz) yeast
300ml (½pt) lukewarm water
2 × 5ml tsp (2tsp) salt
1 × 5ml tsp (1tsp) sugar, 1 egg
about ½kg (1lb 2oz) strong plain
*   flour*

1 Dissolve the yeast in the luke-warm water and add salt, sugar, egg and most of the flour. Work the dough until it is smooth and knead in the rest of the flour with the hands. Cover and let stand in a warm place to rise for about 40 min.
2 Remove the dough to a floured board and divide it into 8 portions. Make buns and place them closely together in a small, greased oven pan about 20 × 25cm (8 × 10in). Place this pan over a saucepan of boiling water, cover with a cloth or poly-thene, then move the saucepan away from the stove. Leave dough to rise again for 20 min.
3 Brush the buns with water or milk and bake for 15–20 min at 220°C, 425°F, Gas 7. Divide the buns with a fork when they have cooled a little. Place them, cut side up, on a baking sheet and put them back into the oven for about 10–12 min at 240°C, 475°F, Gas 9 until they are golden. Cool on a wire rack.

25g (1oz) yeast, 400ml (¾pt) milk
1 × 5ml tsp (1tsp) salt
35g (1½oz) brown sugar
1 × 15ml tbsp (1tbsp) ground
*   caraway seeds*
550g (about 1lb 4oz) finely ground
*   whole rye flour*
whole caraway seeds for decorating

1 Dissolve the yeast in lukewarm milk and add salt, sugar and the crushed caraway seeds. Add the flour and work the dough until smooth.
2 Thoroughly grease a baking tin and spread the dough evenly over the bottom. Mark into squares with a knife dipped in melted butter, cover and leave in a warm place for about 30 min until the dough has almost doubled in bulk.
3 Brush top with water and sprinkle over caraway seeds. Bake for 15 min at 220°C, 425°F, Gas 7.
4 Cool on a wire rack, but break the squares apart before they have cooled completely.

Tea Pastries

(makes 14–16 pastries)
Preparation time: about 20–25 min
Rising time: about 30 min
Baking time: about 12–15 min
Oven temperature: 220°C, 425°F, Gas 7
Middle rack in the oven
Suitable for freezing

25g (1oz) yeast, 150ml (¼pt) milk
2 eggs, 1 × 5ml tsp (1tsp) salt
1 × 5ml tsp (1tsp) sugar
about 300g (11oz) strong plain flour
100g (¼lb) butter or margarine
poppy seeds

1 Dissolve the yeast in cold milk, add 1 egg, salt and sugar. Add flour until the dough is soft and smooth.
2 Roll out the dough immediately on a floured board, place thin slices

Cakes made with Yeast

When you add sugar, butter and perhaps dried fruit to an ordinary dough, the result is fragrant delicious cakes. They are especially good when served freshly baked and still warm. If there are any leftovers, they can be frozen.

The sugar has a stimulating effect on the yeast cells and causes the dough to rise more quickly. Be careful, therefore, not to let the dough rise too long, as it could then collapse during baking. The butter should preferably be rubbed into the flour and not melted. But there are exceptions. Chilled butter can be rolled into dough which has already risen, and the consistency will then be layered, rather like puff pastry. Cakes made with yeast dough are often brushed with egg, cream, coffee, milk, melted butter, sugar syrup, or the like. This gives an attractive, shiny surface, and keeps various kinds of decoration in place. The brushing makes the edges of rolled out dough stick together, so that the filling doesn't seep out during the rising and baking process.

Cakes baked with yeast are very suitable for freezing, but do not put on any icing or decoration until the cakes have been thawed out. Large cakes should be thawed out at room temperature while still in their wrappings, and be heated a little in the oven at about 180°C, 350°F, Gas 4 just before they are to be served; then they will be just as if they were freshly baked. Small cakes can be taken direct from the freezer and thawed in the oven at 190–200°C, 375–400°F, Gas 5–6.

On the following pages are recipes for sweet cakes and buns. Some of the recipes use the same basic dough, but with different fillings, icing and decoration. It is very labour-saving to make one dough and be able to serve two or three different kinds of cakes and buns from it. And everyone, old and young, is fond of this kind of baking.

Nut Cake (below)
1kg (2lb) loaf tin
Preparation time: about 20 min
Rising time: about 1 hr
Baking time: about 35–45 min
Oven temperature: 200–225°C, 400–425°F, Gas 6–7
Lowest rack in the oven
Suitable for freezing

Dough : 600g (1lb 5oz) plain flour
25g (1oz) yeast
250ml (9fl oz) milk
75g (3oz) butter or margarine
75g (3oz) sugar
2 eggs, ½ × 5ml tsp (½tsp) salt
½ lemon
1 egg for brushing top
Filling : 200g (7oz) hazelnuts
85g (3½oz) sugar
1 × 5ml tsp (1tsp) vanilla essence
2 egg whites
egg for brushing

1 Sift the flour into a bowl, make a hollow in the middle and put in the crumbled yeast. Add lukewarm milk and stir lightly without mixing too much flour into the yeast/milk mixture. Sprinkle a thin layer of flour over this 'temporary' dough and put it in a warm place for 15 min.

2 Melt butter, remove the saucepan away from the heat to let the butter cool a little. Stir in the 75g (3oz) sugar, beaten eggs, salt, lemon juice and grated lemon peel.

3 Pour this mixture over flour and yeast in the bowl, stir the dough until it is smooth and even, and let it rise for 20–25 min.

4 Toast the hazel nuts lightly in a dry frying pan. Grind them or chop them finely. Mix the nuts with the sugar, the two egg whites and the vanilla essence. Roll out the dough to a fairly thick oblong, spread the filling lengthwise and brush the edges with beaten egg. Roll the dough together and place in the greased tin. Let the cake rise again for 20–25 min in a warm place, well covered. Brush it with beaten egg and make cuts in the surface to give a diamond pattern. Bake for 35–45 min at 220°C, 425°F, Gas 7 and cool on a wire rack.

Sugar Kringels, Raisin Buns and Small Plaits
(makes 16 buns and 12 kringels or small plaits)
Preparation time: about 15–20 min
Rising time: about 45 min
Baking time: 12–15 min
Oven temperature: 220–240°C, 425–475°F, Gas 7–9
Middle rack in the oven
Suitable for freezing

Dough : 50g (2oz) yeast
100g (¼lb) butter
200ml (7fl oz) milk
2 × 15ml tbsp (2tbsp) sugar
½ × 5ml tsp (½tsp) salt, 1 egg
2 × 15ml tbsp (2tbsp) buttermilk
about ½kg (1lb 2oz) plain flour
Decoration : 4 × 15ml tbsp (4tbsp)
* sugar crystals, poppy seeds*
75g (3oz) raisins

1 Dissolve crumbled yeast in lukewarm milk, not above 35°C (95°F), mixed with melted butter. The liquid must not be over 35°C (95°F).
Add sugar, salt, egg and buttermilk or some other sour milk product and about half the flour. Work the dough with a wooden spoon until it is smooth and knead in the rest of the flour with your hands. Let the

dough stand in a warm place, covered with a cloth or polythene, for 25–30 min to rise.

2 Knead the dough and divide it into two. Knead raisins into one part and shape buns; put on a baking sheet to rise for 15–20 min.

3 Roll out the remaining dough into strips, and shape into kringels (rings or figure eights) or plait three strips together to form small plaited loaves. Put these to rise on a baking sheet and brush with beaten egg. Sprinkle sugar crystals on top of the kringels, and poppy seeds on top of the plaited loaves. Bake for 12–15 min at 220–240°C, 425–475°F, Gas 7–9 and cool on a wire rack. All these can be eaten as they are, or with butter and jam.

Buns
In the illustrations to the right we have rolled out half the Sugar Kringels dough into 16 buns without raisins. They may be baked in the usual way, but can be improved with a little decoration.

1 Roll out round buns and place them on a greased baking sheet or on grease-proof paper.

2 Clip a cross in each bun, at the same time as you 'drag' the scissors a little upwards. Let the buns rise and bake as described in the recipe.

3 When the buns are cold, they can be brushed with melted butter and dipped into sugar crystals, sprinkled with icing sugar, or spread with a thick icing of icing sugar and egg whites.

45

Large Cakes made with Yeast

Party Raisin Bread

Preparation time: about 25 min
Rising time: about 40–45 min
Baking time: about 25 min
Oven temperature: 220°C, 425°F, Gas 7
Middle rack in the oven
Suitable for freezing

125g (4½oz) butter or margarine
100ml (4fl oz) milk
25g (1oz) yeast
2 × 15ml tbsp (2tbsp) sugar
½ × 5ml tsp (½tsp) salt
½ × 5ml tsp (½tsp) cardamom
about 300g (11oz) plain flour
1 egg, 60g (2½oz) raisins,
60g (2½oz) candied peel

1 Melt 1 × 15ml tbsp (1tbsp) butter, add the milk and dissolve the yeast in the lukewarm mixture. Add sugar, salt, cardamom, ½ egg and a good half of the flour. Knead the dough until smooth, set it aside to rise in a warm place, well-covered, until about doubled in bulk.
2 Knead in a little more flour, but the dough must not be too firm. Roll it out, cover with remaining butter and fold, as shown on page 49. Roll out and fold altogether 3 times.
3 Roll out again, sprinkle the candied peel and raisins mixed together over the dough, then roll the dough together and put it into a small round cake tin.

4 Let the cake rise again for about 20 min, brush with egg and bake for 25 min at 220°C, 425°F, Gas 7.

Fig Wreath

Preparation time: about 25 min
Rising time: about 50 min
Baking time: about 30 min
Oven temperature: 200°C, 400°F, Gas 6
Middle rack in the oven
Suitable for freezing

Dough: ½kg (1lb 2oz) plain flour
25–50g (1–2oz) yeast
250ml (9fl oz) milk
75g (3oz) butter or margarine
50g (2oz) sugar
juice and rind of ½ lemon
Filling and decoration:
50–75g (2–3oz) butter or margarine
50g (2oz) sugar
50g (2oz) almonds
50g (2oz) raisins, 100g (¼lb) figs
50g (2oz) chocolate
100g (¼lb) icing sugar

1 Sift the flour into a bowl, crumble the yeast in a hollow in the middle and pour lukewarm milk over it. Dissolve the yeast without mixing in too much of the flour. Sprinkle a little flour on top, cover, and set aside to rise for about 15–20 min.
2 Melt the butter and mix it with sugar, lemon juice and finely grated lemon rind. Pour the mixture into the bowl and work the dough until smooth. Set aside to rise for about 15–20 min.
3 Chop the almonds coarsely and

mix them with the coarsely grated chocolate, chopped figs and raisins.
4 Knead the dough and roll it out to an oblong. Spread the butter for the filling over it and sprinkle the 50g (2oz) sugar, raisins, almonds, chocolate and figs on top. Roll the dough together and cut through it lengthwise with a sharp knife, dipped in flour. Twine the two halves lightly together to form a wreath. Put on a baking sheet to rise again for 15–20 min, and bake for about 30 min at 200°C, 400°F, Gas 6.
5 Stir icing sugar and a little warm water together to make a smooth icing. Ice the cake while it is still warm and put aside to cool.

Advent Wreath

Preparation time: about 15–20 min
Rising time: about 50 min
Baking time: about 25 min
Oven temperature: 220°C, 425°F, Gas 7
Middle rack in the oven
Suitable for freezing

Dough: 300ml (½pt) milk
50g (2oz) yeast
75g (3oz) butter or margarine
5 × 15ml tbsp (5tbsp) sugar
½ × 5ml tsp (½tsp) salt
1 × 5ml tsp (1tsp) cardamom
about ½kg (1lb 2oz) plain flour
Filling: 3–4 × 15ml tbsp (3–4tbsp) butter
3 × 15ml tbsp (3tbsp) sugar
½ × 5ml tsp (½tsp) cinnamon
1 egg for brushing top
50g (2oz) almonds for decoration

Coffee-party Cake with Filling
1 Follow the recipe for Advent Wreath and roll the dough out to fit the baking sheet.
Brush the middle with melted butter and spread the filling over.

2 Fold the dough into three so that all the filling is covered and old in the ends. To prevent the edges from gaping, brush a little beaten egg white along them.

3 Fold the ends under, and place the cake on a greased baking sheet. Let it rise, and brush and bake it, as explained in the Advent Wreath recipe above.

1 Dissolve the yeast in lukewarm milk and stir in melted butter, sugar, salt, cardamom and most of the flour. Work the dough until it is smooth, adding more flour, but do not make it hard. Place in a warm place to rise for about 30 min.

2 Remove the dough to a floured board and roll it out to an oblong shape. Spread softened butter for filling on top and sprinkle sugar, cinnamon and 1–2 × 15ml tbsp (1–2tbsp) chopped almonds over it. Roll the dough together and form it into a wreath on a baking sheet covered with greaseproof paper. Let it rise again for 20 min.

3 Brush the wreath with beaten egg and sprinkle remaining chopped almonds on top. Bake for 25 min at 220°C, 425°F, Gas 7, then cool. If the wreath is to be used with lighted candles, press candle-holders of double tinfoil a little

down into the wreath before it is put in the oven. A large, solid candle with tinfoil wrapped around its base, placed in the middle of the wreath when it has been baked and decorated with non-inflammable greenery, is an attractive variation.

Almond Plait

Preparation time: about 20 min
Rising time: about 1 hr
Baking time: about 30–40 min
Oven temperature: 200–220°C, 400–425°F, Gas 6–7
Lowest rack in the oven
Suitable for freezing

1 quantity dough as for Nut Cake (see page 44)
150g (5oz) almonds
50g (2oz) candied orange or lemon peel
3 × 15ml tbsp (3tbsp) sugar
1 egg for brushing top

Above: An inviting Fig Wreath, filled with almonds, raisins, figs and chocolate.

1 Make the yeast dough as described for Nut Cake. Blanch the almonds, finely chop half of them, and mix with the candied peel. Knead this mixture into the dough before setting it aside to rise.

2 Knead the dough thoroughly after it has finished rising and divide it into three. Roll each third out into a 30cm (12in) long strip. Plait the strips of dough together and fold the ends in. Let the plaits rise again on a greased baking sheet for 20–25 min.

3 Brush the cake with beaten egg. Chop the remaining almonds coarsely and mix them with the sugar. Spread this on top of the cake and bake for 30–40 min at 200–220°C, 400–425°F, Gas 6–7. Cool on a wire rack.

Danish Pastries

Time and care are needed to make Danish Pastries, but the results are especially attractive and delicious.

Danish Pastries (basic dough)

(makes about 32 small Danish Pastries or 2 large)

Preparation time: about 30 min

Resting time for dough: 20–60 min

Rising time: about 20 min

Baking time: (6–8 min for small Danish Pastries, 15–18 min for long bars, wreaths etc

Baking temperature: 220–240°C, 425–475°F, Gas 7–9

Top or middle rack in the oven

Suitable for freezing

A variety of tempting, fresh Danish Pastries.

50g (2oz) yeast
250ml (9fl oz) cold milk
½ × 5ml tsp (½tsp) salt
3 × 15ml tbsp (3tbsp) sugar
1 egg
about ½kg (1lb 2oz) plain flour
To roll out:
250g (9oz) butter
2 × 15ml tbsp (2tbsp) plain flour

1 Dissolve the yeast in the cold milk and add salt, sugar, beaten egg and at least half the flour. Work the dough with a wooden spoon until it is smooth, and knead in the remaining flour, a little at a time. The dough should be smooth but quite soft, so do not handle it any more than is necessary.

2 Roll out the dough as illustrated on page 49 (it is not to rise yet).

3 The dough can now be used in various ways as described in the following recipes. Place the pastries on cold baking sheets, preferably on greaseproof paper as the filling often seeps out. Cover the pastries well and leave to rise for about 20 min in a cool place. Bake as directed, remove carefully from the baking sheets and leave to cool on a wire rack.

Danish Pastries with Fruit Filling

1 quantity basic dough
Filling: 150–200ml (5–7fl oz) fruit purée or thick jam
3–4 × 15ml tbsp (3–4tbsp) cream

1 Roll out the dough to make two oblongs of about 15 × 20cm (6 × 9in). Put apple sauce, apricot jam, preserved prunes, or any other jam or fruit filling in a broad strip in the middle of the dough and turn in the edges as shown in the drawings on page 46.

2 Set the pastries aside to rise, brush the edges with cream and bake

for about 15–18 min at 220°C, 425°F, Gas 7.

3 The pastries can be brushed with a little warm sugar syrup, made of equal parts of sugar and water, if the surface looks a little dry after baking. They can also be sprinkled with a little icing sugar when cold.

Butter Cake
Round cake tin, about 20cm (8in) in diameter
½ quantity of basic dough
Vanilla cream : 2 egg yolks
2 × ml tbsp (2tbsp) sugar
1 × 5ml tsp (1tsp) vanilla sugar
1 × 15ml tbsp (1tbsp) cornflour
200ml (7fl oz) cream
100g (4oz) raisins, 25 almonds

1 Roll out the dough to about 15 × 20cm (6 × 8in). Stir together the egg yolks, sugar, vanilla sugar, cornflour and cream in a heavy saucepan and let the mixture gradually come to the boil, stirring continuously. Remove the saucepan from the heat as soon as the cream is thick and smooth. Beat or stir it from time to time while it is cooling.
2 Spread the cold cream filling lengthwise on the dough to within 2cm (¾in) of the edges. Sprinkle raisins on top and roll the dough together. Cut 2–3cm (¾–1¼in) thick slices and place them with the cut edge up in the greased round cake tin.
3 Set the cake aside to rise, brush with beaten egg and sprinkle almonds on top. Bake at 220°C, 425°F, Gas 7 for about 18–20 min until the cake is golden in colour.

Spandau Cakes
(makes 16 cakes)
½ quantity of basic dough
½ quantity vanilla cream (see Butter Cake, above)
about 60g (2½oz) icing sugar
egg white

1 Roll out the dough to about 30 × 30cm (12 × 12in) and cut it into 16 squares. Fold the points in toward the middle, fasten them with a little egg white, and put a little vanilla cream in the middle.
2 Set the cakes aside to rise on a baking sheet. Brush with milk and bake about 6–8 min at 240°C, 475°F, Gas 9. If you want a shiny surface, brush with a sugar syrup of

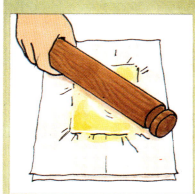

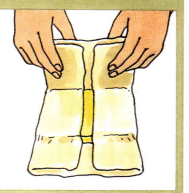

Rolling out Danish Pastry Dough
1 Roll out the dough on a lightly floured board to a square about 40 × 40cm (16 × 16in). Cut chilled butter into thin slices, put them in the middle of the square and sift a thin layer of flour over.
2 Fold the dough in over the butter from the sides, so that you make a parcel.
3 With the open side turned away from you, begin the rolling.

4 Roll the dough out again carefully to its original size, without using too much force. When the butter begins to be visible, fold the dough again in the same way, make a quarter turn with it and roll out again. Fold and roll out two more times. Let the dough preferably stand in a cold place for 10–20 min between each rolling out. Form pastries as in recipe. Place them, covered, on a baking sheet and leave in a cool place for about 20 min to rise.

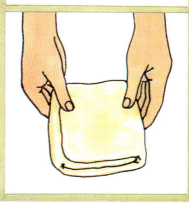

equal parts of icing sugar dissolved in a little egg white.

Stars
(makes 16 stars)
½ quantity of basic dough
Filling : about 100ml (4fl oz) apple sauce or thick jam, egg white, milk for brushing
Icing : about 100g (¼lb) icing sugar, egg white

1 Roll out the dough to about 30 × 30cm (12 × 12in). Cut it into 16 squares and place a spoonful of apple sauce or jam on each.
2 Make a diagonal cut in each corner and fold every other point in over the filling. Brush the points with raw egg white so that they stay in place during baking.
3 Place the stars on a baking sheet to rise, brush with milk and bake for about 6–8 min at 240°C, 475°F, Gas 9. Make an icing of icing sugar and a little raw egg white and drip a little in the middle of each star when they are cold.

Lord Mayor's Cake
1 Place the filling down the middle of the rolled out rectangle of dough.

2 Make diagonal cuts on both sides of the dough, about 2cm (¾in) apart.

3 Fold the strips in over the filling, alternately from the right and left.

Lord Mayor's Cake

½ *quantity basic dough*
100g (¼lb) almonds
100g (¼lb) icing sugar
1 egg (separated)
1 × 15ml tbsp (1tbsp) cream

1 Roll out the dough to a rectangle 15 × 20cm (6 × 8in). Blanch the almonds, flake about a third of them and grind or finely chop the rest. Mix the ground almonds with the icing sugar and egg white and lay the filling in a strip lengthwise on the dough.
2 Make cuts as shown in the diagrams; or fold the dough over the filling, make cuts along the whole length of the dough and draw the cut portions a little out to the side.
3 Set the cake aside to rise, brush with a mixture of egg yolk and cream, and sprinkle the flaked almonds over the top.
Bake at 220°C, 425°F, Gas 7 for about 15–18 min, until the cake is crisp and golden in colour.

Cocks' Combs

(makes about 16 pastries)
½ *quantity basic dough*
75g (3oz) butter or margarine
100g (¼lb) icing sugar
50g (2oz) almonds
1 egg for brushing top
granulated sugar

1 Roll the dough out to a rectangle about 30 × 50cm (12 × 20in). Stir softened butter together with the icing sugar and at least half the blanched and finely chopped almonds.
2 Place the filling in a broad strip in the middle of the rectangle and fold both sides to the centre with a slight overlap. Slice into pieces about 4–5cm (1½–2in) wide and make 4–5 cuts in the top edge of each. Curve the cakes so that the cuts are opened wider.
3 Place the pastries on a baking sheet and set them aside to rise again. Brush with egg and sprinkle top with chopped almonds and granulated sugar. Bake about 6–8 min at 240°C, 475°F, Gas 9.

Cream Buns

(makes 16 buns)
½ *quantity basic dough*
½ *quantity vanilla cream (see Butter Cake, page 49)*
1 egg for brushing top
about 100g (¼lb) icing sugar

1 Roll the dough out into a square about 30 × 30cm (12 × 12in). Cut it into 16 squares and place a little vanilla cream on each.
Fold the corners in over the filling, press them lightly together and place the buns, with the seam underneath, on a baking sheet. Set aside to rise.
2 Brush the buns with beaten egg and bake them until golden at 240°C, 475°F, Gas 9.
3 Brush the warm buns with a little sugar syrup made of equal parts of water and sugar. Sprinkle icing sugar on top.

Birthday Kringel

Preparation time: about 20 min
Rising time: about 50 min
Baking time: about 25–30 min
Oven temperature: 220°C, 425°F, Gas 7
Middle rack in the oven
Suitable for freezing

Dough: 350g (¾lb) plain flour
½ *× 5ml tsp (½tsp) salt*
1 × 5ml tsp (1tsp) cardamom
200g (7oz) butter or margarine
25g (1oz) yeast
100ml (4fl oz) milk, 2 eggs
2 × 15ml tbsp (2tbsp) sugar
Filling and decoration:
100g (¼lb) butter
85g (3½oz) sugar
50g (2oz) almonds
4 × 15ml tbsp (4tbsp) raisins
2 × 15ml tbsp (2tbsp) candied peel
1 egg, sugar crystals

1 Mix flour, salt and cardamom, and rub the butter into the flour with your finger tips. Dissolve the yeast in lukewarm milk and beat the eggs with the sugar. Pour both into the flour, mix the dough with a wooden spoon until it is smooth and elastic and set it aside, covered, in a warm place for about 30 min to rise.
2 Combine the softened butter for the filling with the sugar, 25g (1oz) blanched and finely chopped almonds, raisins and finely chopped

candied peel.

3 Remove the dough to a floured board and knead it. Divide it into two and roll each portion into a rectangle. Place the filling in a strip in the middle and fold the sides in over the filling so that it is covered.

4 Form the pastries into a kringel ring or figure eight on a greased baking sheet. Press the seams tightly together and set the kringel aside to rise for about 20 min. Brush with beaten egg and sprinkle sugar crystals and chopped almonds on top. Bake about 25–30 min at 220°C, 425°F, Gas 7 and cool a little on the baking sheet before transferring to a wire rack.

Jam Pastries
(makes 16 pastries)
½ quantity basic dough
about 150g (5oz) jam
about 100g (¼lb) icing sugar
egg whites, milk for brushing

1 Roll out the dough to a square about 30 × 30cm (12 × 12in) and cut it into 16 squares. Place a little thick jam in the middle of each square, and fold two opposite corners of dough in over the filling. Fasten them with egg white and press them well together.

2 Set the pastries aside on a baking sheet to rise. Brush with milk and bake them for about 6–9 min at 240°C, 475°F, Gas 9 or until they are golden.

3 Decorate the cooled pastries with a glaze of icing sugar dissolved in a little egg white.

Saffron Kringel
Preparation time: about 20 min
Rising time: about 45–50 min
Baking time: about 25 min
Oven temperature: 200–220°C, 400–425°F, Gas 6–7
Lowest rack in the oven
Suitable for freezing

75g (3oz) butter or margarine
250ml (9fl oz) lukewarm milk
25g (1oz) yeast
½ × 5ml tsp (½tsp) salt
3–4 × 15ml tbsp (3–4tbsp) sugar
1 egg
¼ × 5ml tsp (¼tsp) saffron
1 × 15ml tbsp (1tbsp) grated lemon rind
about ½kg (1lb 2oz) plain flour
1 egg yolk for brushing top

1 Melt the butter, add a little of the milk. Dissolve the yeast in the lukewarm mixture.

2 Add salt, sugar, egg, saffron, lemon rind, the remaining milk, and the flour a little at a time. Work the dough until it is smooth and elastic and cover and place in a warm place to rise for about 30 min.

3 Remove the dough to a floured board and divide it into three. Form each portion into a ball and let it stand for 5 min. Roll the balls

Plaited Saffron Kringel, golden and tempting.

out into 50–60cm (20–24in) long 'sausages' and plait them together. Make a ring or figure eight of the plaits and cover and put to rise on a greased baking sheet for 20 min. Brush with the egg yolk beaten with 1 × 15ml tbsp (1tbsp) water. Bake for about 25 min at 200–220°C, 400–425°F, Gas 6–7 and cool on a wire rack.

Filled Crescent Rolls (basic recipe)

(makes about 24 crescents)
Preparation time: about 25 min
Rising time: about 50 min
Baking time: about 15 min
Oven temperature: 200–220°C, 400–425°F, Gas 6–7
Middle rack in the oven
Suitable for freezing without icing and decoration

50g (2oz) yeast
200ml (7fl oz) single cream
1 egg, 1 × 5ml tsp (1tsp) salt
1 × 15ml tbsp (1tbsp) sugar
25ml (1fl oz) sour cream
100g (¼lb) butter or margarine
about ½kg (1lb 2oz) plain flour

1. Dissolve the yeast in lukewarm cream and add egg, salt, sugar and sour cream. Rub the butter into about 400g (14oz) flour, pour the yeast mixture over and knead the dough until elastic, adding a little more flour. Cover and put aside to rise for about 30 min.

2 Remove the dough to a floured board and roll out. Cut out triangles and put filling on each. Roll up from the broadest side, bend the crescents into a curve and place them on a greased baking sheet with the point of the dough facing down. Let them rise again for 20 min. Bake according to directions and place on a wire rack to cool.

Suggestions for filling: Cinnamon Crescents

Stir together 50g (2oz) softened butter, 50g (2oz) sugar and ½ × 15ml tbsp (½tbsp) cinnamon. Fill the crescents, roll up, brush with

as directed and cool. Make a thick glazing of 100g (4oz) icing sugar and the rest of the egg white. Spread the icing on the crescents.

Mocha Crescents

Stir together a filling made of 2 × 15ml tbsp (2tbsp) softened butter, 3 × 15ml tbsp (3tbsp) sugar, 1 × 5ml tsp (1tsp) cocoa and 1 × 15ml tbsp (1tbsp) instant coffee. Fill the crescents, roll up, and bake. Decorate the cooled crescents with an icing made of about 100g (¼lb) icing sugar and a little strong coffee.

Shrovetide Buns

(makes 20–25 buns)
Preparation time: about 30 min
Rising time: about 1 hr
Baking time: 12–15 min
Oven temperature: 220–230°C, 425–450°F, Gas 7–8
Middle rack in the oven
Suitable for freezing, without cream

Dough:
75g (3oz) butter or margarine
300ml (½pt) milk
25g (1oz) yeast
4 × 15ml tbsp (4tbsp) sugar
½ × 5ml tsp (½tsp) salt, 1 egg yolk
about ½kg (1lb 2oz) plain flour
Filling and decoration:
150g (5oz) almonds
2 egg whites
4 × 15ml tbsp (4tbsp) milk
85g (3½oz) sugar
1 egg yolk for brushing top
½ litre (about 1pt) whipping cream
icing sugar

1 Melt the butter and stir in the warm milk.
Dissolve the yeast in about 100ml (4fl oz) of the lukewarm liquid and add salt, sugar, egg yolk, the rest of the lukewarm milk and most of the flour. Stir the dough thoroughly and add more flour until the dough is smooth and not too firm. Cover and set aside in a warm place for 30–35 min to rise.
2 Remove the dough to a floured board and divide and shape it into even-sized buns. Let these rise again under a cloth or polythene on a greased baking sheet for 25–30 min.
3 Brush with egg yolk beaten with 1 × 15ml tbsp (1tbsp) water or milk. Bake for 12–15 min at 220–230°C, 425–450°F, Gas 7–8 and cool on a wire rack.

4 Cut the top off the buns, take out barely half the inside and moisten this with the milk for filling. Beat egg whites until stiff and carefully mix in the blanched and ground almonds and the moist inside of the buns. Spread this filling in the buns, put whipped cream on top of each and place the 'lid' loosely on top. Sift icing sugar over the tops.

Berlin Buns (left)

(makes 20–24 buns)
Preparation time: about 20–25 min
Rising time: about 50–55 min
Baking time: about 5–6 min per bun
Suitable for freezing

50g (2oz) yeast, 150ml (¼pt) milk
1 × 5ml tsp (1tsp) salt
40g (1½oz) sugar
2 × 15ml tbsp (2tbsp) oil
2 × 15ml tbsp (2tbsp) rum or lemon juice
1 egg + 1 egg yolk
about ½kg (1lb 2oz) plain flour
jam or crushed fruit
oil or lard for deep-frying
sugar or icing sugar

1 Dissolve the yeast in lukewarm milk and add salt, sugar, oil, rum or lemon juice and the beaten egg and egg yolk. Add the flour a little at a time, stir thoroughly as long as the dough is sticky, then knead in the rest of the flour by hand. Cover and leave in a warm place for 30–35 min to rise.
2 Remove the dough to a floured board and roll it out into two rectangles about 1cm (½in) thick. With a glass, outline rounds of 6–7cm (about 2½in) diameter on the one rectangle of dough and put 1–2 × 5ml tsp (1–2tsp) jam in the middle of each round. Lay the other rectangle of dough on top and press the glass through both layers of dough. Use a glass with quite thick edges, as then the cakes will stick together better during the baking.
3 Cover and let the buns stand in a warm place to rise for about 20 min. Heat oil or lard in a saucepan to 175–180°C (350–360°F) or until a cube of bread turns pale brown in 1 min. Put in 3–4 buns at a time and cook them until light brown.
4 Remove the buns with a slotted spoon and drain on kitchen paper. Roll them in sugar or icing sugar and serve them hot or lukewarm.

beaten egg and sprinkle cinnamon and sugar crystals on top. Bake as directed.

Apple Crescents

Put 1–2 × 5ml tsp (1–2tsp) thick apple sauce on the triangles. Roll them up, bake according to directions, and sprinkle over a thin layer of icing sugar.

Marzipan Crescents

Stir 100g (¼lb) grated marzipan with about ½ a raw egg white. Spread the filling on the crescents, roll up, bake

Cakes to Cut into Slices

Crumble Cake with Apricots (above); Tosca Cake (below).

Basic Dough
1 shallow tin, 30 × 40cm (12 × 16in)
Preparation time: about 15 min
Rising time: about 30 min
Baking time and oven temperature:
see recipes
Middle rack in the oven
Suitable for freezing

½kg (1 lb 2oz) plain flour
150g (5oz) butter or margarine
3 × 15ml tbsp (3 tbsp) sugar
grated rind of ½ lemon
50g (2oz) yeast
250ml (9 fl oz) milk

1 Sift the flour into a bowl and rub in the butter with your finger tips. Sprinkle in sugar and lemon rind.
2 Dissolve the yeast in lukewarm milk, pour it into the flour mixture and stir the dough until it is smooth and elastic. Put a cloth or polythene over the bowl and let the dough rise in a warm place until it has doubled in bulk.
3 Line the tin with greaseproof paper. Knead the dough after it has finished rising and place it in the tin.
4 This base can be left to rise for 20 min on its own, or the filling can be spread over the top right away and the complete cake baked.

Crumble Cake with Apricots
Preparation time: about 25 min
Rising time: about 30 min
Baking time: about 20–25 min
Oven temperature: 200°C, 400°F, Gas 6
Suitable for freezing

1 quantity Basic Dough
2 large cans of apricots
250g (9oz) plain flour
200g (7oz) sugar
2 × 5ml tsp (2 tsp) vanilla sugar
200g (7oz) butter or margarine

1 Make the dough and place in greased or greaseproof paper lined tin. Drain the apricots well.
2 Mix flour, sugar and vanilla sugar. Rub in chilled butter with the tips of your fingers, or melt it and drip it into the flour mixture, stirring all the while, so that the mixture is crumbly.
3 Place the apricots, round side up, on top of the yeast dough and spread the crumble on top. Let the cake rise again for 15–20 min, or bake it right away. Cool and slice.

Cream Cake with Peaches
(right)

Preparation time: about 25–30 min
Rising time: about 40 min
Baking time: about 35–40 min
Oven temperature: 200–220°C,
400–425°F, Gas 6–7

1 quantity Basic Dough
2 large cans of halved peaches
400g (14oz) cottage cheese
3 eggs
3 × 15ml tbsp (3tbsp) cornflour
4 × 15ml tbsp (4tbsp) sugar
½ lemon, 50g (2oz) almonds

1 Make the dough and put it in the greased or lined tin. Drain the peaches well through a sieve.
2 Stir cottage cheese with beaten eggs, cornflour, sugar, lemon juice and grated lemon rind.
3 Spread the cheese mixture over the dough and place the peaches on top. Sprinkle blanched, chopped almonds over and let the cake rise for 10 min. Bake, and cut into slices when cool.

Tosca Cake

Preparation time: about 20 min
Rising time: about 30 min
Baking time: 20–25 min
Oven temperature: 220°C, 425°F,
Gas 7
Suitable for freezing

1 quantity Basic Dough
200g (7oz) butter or margarine
125–150g (4½–5oz) almonds
100g (¼lb) sugar
2 × 5ml tsp (2tsp) vanilla sugar

1 Make the dough and put it in the greased or paper-lined tin. Prick with a fork, so that bubbles will not form during the baking.
2 Cut chilled butter into slices and lay these on top of the dough. Blanch the almonds, flake them and sprinkle them over the butter. Sprinkle sugar and vanilla sugar on top. Bake, and cut into slices when cool.

Cream Slice with Crisp Meringue (right)

Preparation time: about 25 min
Rising time: about 40 min
Baking time: about 30–40 min
Oven temperature: 200–220°C,
400–425°F, Gas 6–7
Suitable for freezing

1 quantity Basic Dough
125g (4½oz) butter or margarine
3 eggs, separated
175g (6oz) sugar
1 lemon, 200g (7oz) almonds

1 Make the yeast dough and put it into the greased or lined tin. Let it rise again for about 10 min.
2 Mix softened butter very gradually with egg yolks, blanched and finely chopped almonds, 100g (¼lb) sugar and finely grated lemon rind. Spread the mixture over the dough. Beat the egg whites until stiff, fold in the remaining sugar and spread this meringue over the creamy filling. The meringue mixture and the butter cream can also be mixed and spread over the cake together.
Bake according to directions and cut the cake into slices when cold.

2 Beat butter and sugar until light and fluffy and stir in the egg yolks one at a time. Add raisins, lemon juice and rind, cream and about 150g (5oz) flour.

3 Stir in the yeast mixture and add flour to the dough until it is soft and elastic. Beat the egg whites until they are very stiff and fold them carefully into the dough.

4 Put the dough into the well-greased and floured mould, cover with a damp cloth or polythene and let it rise for about 1 hr. Bake as directed. Test the cake with a thin wooden skewer, the cake is ready when the skewer comes out dry. Turn onto a wire rack to cool.

Cinnamon Cake with Apples

1 deep, ring mould
Preparation time: about 20 min
Rising time: about 1½ hr
Baking time: 1–1¼ hr
Oven temperature: 180–190°C, 350–375°F, Gas 4–5
Lowest rack in the oven
Suitable for freezing

50g (2oz) yeast
200ml (7fl oz) milk
½kg (1lb 2oz) plain flour
125g (4½oz) butter or margarine
100g (¼lb) brown sugar
1 × 5ml tsp (1tsp) cinnamon
½ × 5ml tsp (½tsp) ginger
½ × 5ml tsp (½tsp) powdered cloves
1 egg, 2 apples (150–200g, 5–7oz)

1 Dissolve the yeast in 100ml (4fl oz) lukewarm milk. Rub the butter into the flour and add sugar and spices.

2 Pour the yeast mixture and the beaten egg into the flour. Knead the dough and add more milk until it is soft and elastic. Add the peeled, grated apples and leave dough aside to rise until doubled in bulk.

3 Knead the dough lightly and put it into the well-greased, floured tin. Let rise again for about 30 min, then bake as directed. Cool on a wire rack.

Sister Cake

1 deep, ring mould
Preparation time: about 15 min
Rising time: about 1 hr
Baking time: about 45–40 min
Oven temperature: 200°C, 400°F, Gas 6
Lowest rack in the oven
Suitable for freezing

Cakes baked in a Ring Mould

Gugelhupf

1 deep ring mould
Preparation time: about 25 min
Rising time: about 1 hr
Baking time: about 40–45 min
Oven temperature: 200–220°C, 400–425°F, Gas 6–7
Lowest rack in the oven
Suitable for freezing

about 60g (2½oz) raisins
3 × 15ml tbsp (3tbsp) rum
50g (2oz) yeast
100ml (4fl oz) milk
200g (7oz) butter or margarine
5 egg yolks
125g (4½oz) sugar
3 egg whites
½ lemon, 2 × 15ml tbsp (2tbsp) cream
about 400g (14oz) plain flour

1 Soak the raisins in the rum. Dissolve the yeast in lukewarm milk.

150g (5oz) butter, 50g (2oz) sugar
1 egg, 25g (1oz) yeast
150ml (¼pt) milk
350g (¾lb) plain flour
1 × 5ml tsp (1tsp) cardamom
60g (2½oz) raisins
2 × 15ml tbsp (2tbsp) candied peel
icing sugar

1 Stir the butter and sugar until light and fluffy, then stir in the egg together with 1–2 × 15ml tbsp (1–2tbsp) flour. Dissolve the yeast in lukewarm milk.

2 Stir the yeast liquid into the butter mixture and add remaining flour, cardamom, raisins and chopped candied peel. Work the dough until it is smooth and elastic and put it into the greased and floured tin.

3 Cover the tin with a damp cloth or polythene and let the dough rise for 1 hr in a warm place. Bake as directed. Turn the cake out onto a wire rack and sift icing sugar on top.

Chocolate Ring

1 deep, ring mould
Preparation time: about 25 min
Rising time: about 35–40 min
Baking time: about 40–50 min
Oven temperature: 180°C, 350°F, Gas 4
Lowest rack in the oven
Suitable for freezing before icing

350g (¾lb) plain flour
25g (1oz) yeast
100ml (4fl oz) milk
100g (¼lb) sugar
3 eggs
175g (6oz) butter or margarine
½ lemon, 150g (5oz) currants
Icing: 2 × 15ml tbsp (2tbsp) butter
100g (¼lb) chocolate
blanched almonds or other nuts for
   decoration

1 Sift the flour into a bowl and put the crumbled yeast into a hollow in the middle. Pour lukewarm milk over and dissolve the yeast with a little of the flour. Put the bowl in a warm place, covered, for 15 min, so that the yeast mixture rises.

2 Work in the sugar, the beaten eggs, softened butter, grated lemon rind into the flour so that the dough becomes soft and elastic. Set aside to rise for 20–25 min.

3 Meanwhile, rinse the currants in warm water and dry them well. Work them quickly into the dough and fill it into the well-greased and floured ring mould. Bake as directed and turn out onto a wire rack to cool.

4 Break the chocolate into pieces and melt over hot water, then add the butter and stir until shiny. Spread the icing carefully over the cake and let it harden in a cool place. Decorate with almonds or other nuts before the icing has hardened.

Chocolate Ring is delightful – both in taste and appearance.

From Far-off Places

Many countries have traditions and specialities in yeast baking. Here is a selection.

Poppy Cake (opposite)
1kg (2lb) loaf tin
Preparation time: about 30 min
Rising time: about 1 hr
Baking time: about 30–40 min
Oven temperature: 200°C, 400°F, Gas 6
Lowest rack in the oven
Suitable for freezing

Dough : about 25g (1oz) yeast
300ml (½pt) milk
1 egg, 100g (¼lb) sugar
1 × 5ml tsp (1tsp) salt
75g (3oz) butter or margarine
about ½kg (1lb 2oz) plain flour
Filling : 100g (¼lb) poppy seeds
about 200ml (7fl oz) single cream
25g (1oz) almonds
4 × 15ml tbsp (4tbsp) sugar
1 × 5ml tsp (1tsp) vanilla sugar
2 × 15ml tbsp (2tbsp) butter
1 egg for brushing top

1 Dissolve the yeast in lukewarm milk and stir in the egg, sugar, salt, melted butter and most of the flour. Work the dough with a wooden spoon until it is smooth and knead in more flour with your hands. The dough should be fairly soft. Cover and set aside in a warm place to rise until just about doubled in bulk.

2 Grind the poppy seeds in a mortar. Grind the almonds, mix them with the poppy seeds in a saucepan, place over low heat and add cream, a little at a time, until the mixture is about as thick as porridge. Stir in sugar, vanilla sugar and butter.

3 Knead the dough lightly, roll it out and spread the filling on top. Roll the dough together and put into the greased tin. Let the cake rise again for 20–25 min. Brush with beaten egg, make a cut lengthwise with a sharp knife, and bake as directed. Cool on a wire rack.

VARIATION

Instead of poppy seeds, the cake can be filled with a nut cream, as on the left of the picture. The cream is made of 100g (¼lb) nuts, finely chopped or ground. Add egg white a little at a time until the cream is smooth. Sweeten with icing sugar and flavour with a little rum or liqueur. Coffee liqueur gives a very good flavour to this cake.

Savarin (opposite right)
1 deep, ring mould
Preparation time: about 25 min
Rising time: about ¾ hr
Baking time: about 25–30 min
Oven temperature: 200–220°C, 400–425°F, Gas 6–7
Middle rack in the oven
Suitable for freezing without filling

Dough:
175g (6oz) butter or margarine
25g (1oz) yeast
100ml (4fl oz) single cream, 4 eggs
2 × 15ml tbsp (2tbsp) sugar
½ × 5ml tsp (½tsp) salt
250g (9oz) plain flour
Sugar syrup: 250ml (9fl oz) water
200g (7oz) sugar
2–3 × 15ml tbsp (2–3tbsp) orange liqueur

1 Melt the butter and cool it a little. Add the cream and dissolve crumbled yeast in the mixture. Add the eggs, one at a time, stirring well between each addition. Then stir in sugar, salt and flour. Work the dough until smooth. Cover with a damp cloth or polythene and put it aside to rise in a warm place for 40–45 min.
2 Boil sugar and water together for 15–20 min to make the syrup. It should be thick, but the sugar must not be allowed to crystallise. Remove the saucepan from the heat and add the liqueur.
3 Lightly knead the dough which has now finished rising, and put it into the well-greased mould. Bake as directed, turn the cake out carefully onto a wire rack and wash the tin.
4 Put the cake back into the tin and prick holes all over it with, for example, a knitting needle. Pour the sugar syrup over little by little, so that the cake will absorb it gradually. Let the cake stand in a cool place for at least 2–3 hr.
5 Turn the cake out onto a serving dish and fill it with cut-up fresh fruit which has been lying in a marinade of sweet white wine or sugar syrup with a little liqueur added.

Baba au Rhum
1 ring mould
Preparation time: about 20 min
Rising time: about 1 hr
Baking time: about 30 min
Oven temperature: 220 and 180°C, 425 and 350°F, Gas 7 and 4

Middle rack in the oven
Suitable for freezing but quality will suffer a little

Dough: 25g (1oz) yeast
100ml (4fl oz) milk
4 eggs, 2 × 15ml tbsp (2tbsp) sugar
½ × 5ml tsp (½tsp) salt
vanilla essence
350g (¾lb) plain flour
1 × 15ml tbsp (1tbsp) white rum
100g (¼lb) butter or margarine
Sugar syrup: 250ml (9fl oz) water
250g (9oz) sugar
2–3 × 15ml tbsp (2–3tbsp) white rum

1 Dissolve the yeast in lukewarm milk. Beat the eggs with the sugar and stir in the yeast mixture, together with the salt, vanilla essence to taste, flour and rum. Stir this soft dough until elastic, put butter in slivers on top and put the dough, covered, in a warm place to rise.
2 Knead the dough with the butter which should now be half melted, and put it into the well-greased and floured ring mould. Let it rise again for about 20 min. Bake for 10 min at 220°C, 425°F, Gas 7 and then at 180°C, 350°F, Gas 4 until the cake is baked through.
3 Make a thick sugar syrup of water and sugar, turn off the heat and add the rum. Turn the cake out onto a wire rack and wash the mould.
Put the cake back into the mould immediately after cooling and, using a knitting needle, prick it all over with small holes. Drip the rum syrup over the cake several times.
4 Cool the cake and let it stand for 2–3 hr to absorb the syrup thoroughly. Serve it with whipped or sour cream.

Baking on a Large Scale

There is every reason to start baking on a grand scale when you have flour at hand and the oven is warm – and you have the time and the energy. Allow 3 hr, roll up your sleeves and follow the time-table below.

The following is a good selection for this large-scale bake:
2 coarse Farmer's Bread loaves (see page 17)
2 Round Wheat Bread (see page 37)
1 large yeast wreath (the recipe for the Advent Wreath is on pages 46–7) and/or 24 buns with different filling.
There will be time enough for both the Advent Wreath and the buns, if you want to make them. Make a double quantity of dough, and make the bread doughs about ½ hr later than the recipe states.

When you have done large-scale baking a couple of times, you will be experienced enough to exchange one recipe with another and still keep to the time-table.

Before You Start
Read through the recipes carefully and check that you have everything you need at hand.
Have everything standing in the kitchen for a while – ingredients, bowls etc, so that everything is at room temperature. It is very important that nothing that you are going to use is cold. Be sure to have ready either greaseproof paper or melted butter and brush for greasing warm baking sheets.

Suggestions for Fillings:
1 100g (¼lb) ground almonds mixed with 40g (1½oz) icing sugar and ½–1 egg white.

2 3 × 15ml tbsp (3tbsp) softened butter or margarine, mixed with 3 × 15ml tbsp (3tbsp) icing sugar, 1 × 15ml tbsp (1tbsp) cinnamon and 60g (2½oz) raisins.

3 150ml (¼pt) thick apple sauce or thick jam.

4 3 × 15ml tbsp (3tbsp) softened butter or margarine, mixed with 3 × 15ml tbsp (3tbsp) icing sugar, 1 × 15ml tbsp (1tbsp) grated lemon rind and 1–2 × 5ml tsp (1–2tsp) vanilla sugar.

5 2 × 15ml tbsp (2tbsp) butter or margarine, 60g (2½oz) raisins and 40g (1½oz) chopped candied peel.

First Hour
First make the dough for the Advent Wreath and/or the buns, and put it aside to rise for about 30 min.
Make a double quantity of basic dough for the Round Wheat Bread and set it to rise for about 45 min.

Raisins and Candied Peel Buns

Filled Buns

Clipped Buns

Knead Filling No 5 into a quantity of dough, form buns, let them rise again and brush with egg yolk.
All buns are cooked at 230–240°C, 450–475°F, Gas 8–9.

Form the buns, make a hollow and put in 1 × 5ml tsp (1tsp) of Filling No 1. Pull the dough over the filling, allow to rise again, brush with egg and sprinkle coarse sugar crystals on top.

Roll out the dough to a rectangle and spread on Filling No 4. Cut slices and clip three incisions in each. Fold the incisions outward a little, let dough rise again and brush with egg.

Note the exact time for each dough, it is so easy to forget when the dough has been put aside to rise.

Make the filling for the Advent Wreath. Choose one or several kinds of filling for the buns and get everything ready. Make dough for Farmer's Bread, and put it to rise.

Remove the dough for the Advent Wreath to a floured board and roll it out into a rectangle. Fill it and form a wreath, and put this aside to rise again on a baking sheet. Or divide the dough into 24 pieces if you want to make filled buns.

Second Hour

Heat the oven and set the thermostat at 220°C, 425°F, Gas 7. Fill and shape the buns (see detailed drawings at the foot of the page). Set them aside to rise for about 12–15 min.

Remove the Wheat Bread dough to a floured board, divide it into two and form round or oblong loaves as you wish. Set them on a greased baking sheet to rise again for 20–25 min.

Brush and sprinkle the Advent Wreath or the buns with coarse sugar crystals, and put on baking sheets in the oven on the middle rack. The buns may be baked at about 240°C, 475°F, Gas 9 for 12–15 min.

Remove the dough for the Farmer's Bread to a floured board, divide it into two and form round loaves and set aside to rise again on a greased baking sheet for about 30 min.

The Advent Wreath should now have finished baking and can be taken out of the oven.

Third Hour

Turn the thermostat down to 200–220°C, 400–425°F, Gas 6–7. Brush the Wheat Bread loaves and put them in the oven on the lowest rack. While the wheat loaves are baking in the oven, you will have plenty of time to begin to tidy up and wash everything before the Farmer's Bread loaves need to be brushed on top and baked.

Remove the Wheat Bread loaves when they have finished baking and put them on a rack to cool.

Brush over the tops of the Farmer's Bread loaves and bake them. Begin to wrap up the baked products which are to be frozen before they have cooled completely.

	Time-table for Large-scale Baking					
	Advent Wreath		**Wheat Bread**		**Farmer's Bread**	
1st hr	00	} Make dough	00	} Make dough	00	
	10		10		10	
	20	} 1st rising	20		20	
	30	} Make filling	30		30	} Make dough
	40		40	} 1st rising	40	
	50	} Form wreath	50		50	
	60		60		60	} 1st rising
2nd hr		} 2nd rising	10	} Form loaves	10	
	10		20	} 2nd rising	20	
	20	} Brushing and baking	30		30	} Form loaves
	30		40	} Brushing and baking	40	
	40		50		50	} 2nd rising
	50		60		60	
	60					
3rd hr	10		10		10	
	20		20		20	} Brushing and baking
	30		30		30	
	40		40		40	
	50		50		50	
	60		60		60	

Raisin Snails

Twisted Buns

Roll out the dough to a rectangle and spread on Filling No 2. Roll up, cut slices and turn in the ends. Leave to rise again, brush with sugared water and sprinkle sugar on top.

Roll out the dough to a rectangle and spread on Filling No 2 or No 3. Roll up, twist the roll a quarter turn, cut slices and twist them. Allow to rise, brush with egg and sprinkle on sugar.

61

Storing Bread and Other Baked Products

Yeast baking tastes best the same day as it is made. But there are not many people who have time to bake every day, and if you want to preserve the taste and consistency as nearly as possible, it is important to store it correctly.

Bread Bin or Refrigerator?

Breads containing a lot of finer flour, such as white bread, rolls, buns etc, can be kept for 1–3 days in a plastic bag in the bread bin.

When this bread begins to appear old and dry, it is due partly to drying out and partly to changes in the content of the starch. This occurs most rapidly at 2–3°C (36–37°F) and therefore this kind of baked product should never be kept in the refrigerator.

Coarser types of bread such as rye bread and the like can, on the other hand, keep for over a week, tightly wrapped in plastic in the refrigerator. The bread becomes a little firmer in consistency and easier to cut than when it was newly baked. Bread baked of sourdough or the coarsest types of flour keeps fresh even longer than ordinary rye bread. Dinner rolls, hard rolls, crescents etc can be freshened up by brushing them with cold water and putting them into the oven for a few minutes at 200–220°C, 400–425°F, Gas 6–7.

The formation of mould on baked products can be a problem, especially in summer time. Mould fungus thrives in warmth and dampness, and it is therefore very important that all baked products are completely cooled before they are put into the bread bin. Always put your baking on a wire rack to cool, this allows the dampness and heat to escape as quickly as possible. Never eat mouldy bread, and do not let animals eat it either. Mould is not directly poisonous, but it can cause stomach discomforts.

The Freezer

Freezing is absolutely the best way to store bread and other baked products. At minus. 18–25°C (0 to −12°F) almost all development in baked products stops, and the baked goods seem almost freshly baked when they are thawed. Light types of bread are packed in deep-freeze wrappings while they are lukewarm, then are cooled completely and put into the freezer. The reason for wrapping the bread while it is lukewarm is that then the crust doesn't fall off so easily from the rest of the bread when it is thawed.

It is best to freeze breads which have been completely baked, but it is possible to freeze bread which has been just shaped and risen. However, the bread must then be made with a double quantity of yeast.

If you do not use very much bread, it may pay you to divide large loaves or cut slices, and thus freeze one or two days' supply.

Wrapping

Special heavy aluminium foil containers are available in different sizes and shapes for baking and freezing.

Bread and cakes can be baked in these moulds, which do not need to be greased. After the baked products have been cooled, the moulds are put into plastic bags especially suited for freezing, and closed with clips or tape. With careful use the moulds can be used several times. Plastic foil in rolls or bags, especially intended for freezing, makes good wrappings for yeast baking. You can write with a pen on the special freezing tape. It is very important to write the freezing date on all baked products.

Do not use ordinary plastic bags for freezing, they are too thin and the baked products can dry out and be frost damaged.

Large cakes, kringels, Danish pastries and the like should be protected with a piece of cardboard underneath. This is to avoid breakage or damage when you move baked goods in the freezer.

Freezing Process

It is important to freeze baked goods as quickly as possible in order to retain their freshness and taste. Set the thermostat on the freezer or freezing compartment to coldest, well ahead of time. Put the baked goods in the coldest section or as near the freezing elements as possible.

The temperature should preferably be at least minus −25°C (−12°F).

How Long to Keep in Freezer

Bread with very little fat content keeps well for about 6 months when the temperature in the freezer or freezing compartment is at least −18°C (0°F).

Cakes, raw dough and breads with high fat content should not be kept for more than 3–4 months, at the above-mentioned temperature.

Thawing-out

Whole loaves and cakes are best thawed out in their wrappings at room temperature. An exception to this rule is French Bread which is best thawed in the oven at 220–240°C, 425–475°F, Gas 7–9 for 8–10 min. Bread which has been thawed can be heated for 5–10 min in the oven at 200°C, 400°F, Gas 6 to freshen up the crust, but note that bread that has been frozen dries out more quickly than freshly baked bread.

Buns, small dinner rolls and the like should be thawed in their wrappings at room temperature or in the oven. Bread which has been frozen in slices should be thawed in its wrappings in the refrigerator.

Thawing out frozen baked goods:

At room temperature:

Whole loaves and large cakes	3–5 hr
Sliced bread	15–20 min
Buns, hard rolls and similar	30–60 min

In the oven (approximate time):

Whole loaves 45 min at 180°C, 350°F, Gas 4
Large cakes 25 min at 200°C, 400°F, Gas 6
Small loaves 10 min at 200°C, 400°F, Gas 6

Rapid thawing:

In an emergency you can put frozen slices of bread in the toaster for a couple of minutes.

Index